DEBATING RESTOR

Debating
the oppc — y to offer contrasting
topics of contemporary, general interest.

In this first volume of the series, Carolyn Ho
munities and the state should be more restorative
harms caused by crimes, antisocial behaviour and oth civilities.
She supports the exclusive use of restorative justice for many
non-serious offences, and favours approaches that, by integrating
restorative and retributive philosophies, take restorative practices
into the 'deep end' of criminal justice. While acknowledging that
restorative justice appears to have much to offer in terms of
criminal justice reform, Chris Cunneen offers a different account,
contending that the theoretical cogency of restorative ideas is limited by their lack of a coherent analysis of social and political power.
He goes on to argue that after several decades of experimentation,
restorative justice has not produced significant change in the criminal justice system and that the attempt to establish it as a feasible
alternative to dominant practices of criminal justice has failed. This
lively and valuable debate will be of great interest to everyone interested in the criminal justice system.

Volume 1 in the series Debating Law

Debating Law

General Editor: Professor Peter Cane, the Australian National University. Debating Law is a new, exciting series edited by Peter Cane that gives scholarly experts the opportunity to offer contrasting perspectives on significant topics of contemporary, general interest.

Debating Restorative Justice

Chris Cunneen
and
Carolyn Hoyle

·HART·
PUBLISHING

OXFORD – PORTLAND OREGON
2010

Published in the United Kingdom by Hart Publishing Ltd
16C Worcester Place, Oxford, OX1 2JW
Telephone: +44 (0)1865 517530
Fax: +44 (0)1865 510710
E-mail: mail@hartpub.co.uk
Website: http://www.hartpub.co.uk

Published in North America (US and Canada) by
Hart Publishing
c/o International Specialized Book Services
920 NE 58th Avenue, Suite 300
Portland, OR 97213-3786
USA
Tel: +1 503 287 3093 or toll-free: (1) 800 944 6190
Fax: +1 503 280 8832
E-mail: orders@isbs.com
Website: http://www.isbs.com

British Library Cataloguing in Publication Data
Data Available

ISBN: 978-1-84946-022-4

Typeset by Hope Services, Abingdon
Printed and bound in Great Britain by
TJ International Ltd, Padstow, Cornwall

Series Editors Preface

This innovative and exciting series was inspired by one of the best-known philosophy books of the latter half of the twentieth century. *Utilitarianism for and against* by JJC Smart and Bernard Williams, published in 1973, is described on its cover as '[t]wo essays…written from opposite points of view'. It is one of the classics of the modern literature on utilitarianism.

Based on this model, books in the *Debating Law* series will contain two essays of around 30,000 words, each developing a strong and intellectually rigorous argument on a topic of contemporary and ongoing debate. The aim is to stimulate, challenge and inform by bringing contrasting perspectives together in the one volume.

The *Debating Law* series offers a forum for scholarly argument and advocacy. It gives essayists the opportunity to make a fresh and provocative statement of a normative position freed from a tight requirement of 'balance'. Although debaters are encouraged to exchange ideas during the writing process, it is not the intention that the two essays will answer one another but rather that each will provide an independent statement of a point of view. Authors may take different tacks and address different issues within the broad topic, and the starting points or foundations of the case on one side may be different from those of the case on the other side. The confident expectation is that the debate format will sharpen issues, and highlight areas of both agreement and disagreement, in an effective and illuminating way.

The *Debating Law* series is designed for a wide readership. The aim is that each essay should be self-contained, accessibly written and only lightly endnoted. Books in the series will be valuable for those coming to the topic for the first time and also for the experienced reader seeking a stimulating, thought-provoking and concise statement of different points of view. They will provide valuable resources for teaching as well as lively discussions of important issues of wide current interest.

Peter Cane

Acknowledgements by Carolyn Hoyle

Some of the arguments in my essay draw on previous articles I have written alone or with colleagues. I am grateful to them and to the vibrant intellectual life of the Oxford Centre for Criminology for providing encouragement and inspiration. Over the last decade my thinking about restorative justice has benefited from conversations with my Oxford colleagues, Lucia Zedner and Andrew Ashworth, as well as with undergraduate and postgraduate students, in particular those in my Restorative Justice course in the MSc in Criminology and Criminal Justice. I am grateful to my current and former students—particularly Brett Hartley, Mark Walters and Stephan Noguera—for research assistance and, more importantly, for pointing out contradictions in my arguments.

I am indebted to Richard Young with whom I carried out years of research into restorative justice and co-authored many essays. In particular, the discussion on punishment draws on a chapter which we wrote together but which built on his reflections on the penal philosophies in evidence in restorative encounters.

I am grateful to Peter Cane and to my husband, David Rose, both of whom commented on—and certainly improved—an earlier draft. And, finally, I dedicate the essay to my wonderful children, Jacob and Daniel Rose. As energetic boys of 10 and 6 they test my restorative principles to the limit. At the end of this long essay, I confess that Jacob, in particular, knows that sometimes I fail to put my restorative principles into practice, and denigrate rather than reintegrate!

Acknowledgements by Chris Cunneen

Discussions about restorative justice always seem to arouse passionate responses and over the last twenty years or so I have had the pleasure of engaging in and learning from many formal and informal debates with a wide variety of people. I want to particularly acknowledge the work of Harry Blagg, Kathy Daly and Julie Stubbs whose insights and scholarship have influenced the development of my own ideas. I have also spoken, in various contexts, with many people who were offenders or victims of crime—their views have also been important in clarifying my own ideas. Of course neither my colleagues nor the unwilling participants in the criminal justice system should be held accountable for the arguments expressed in this book.

My contribution to this book would not have been possible without the excellent work of my research associate Ms Fiona Allison. Peter Cane provided helpful comments on the draft text. As always, my partner Kate was supportive well beyond what any reasonable person might expect.

Contents

The Case for Restorative Justice

I. INTRODUCTION

EARLY WRITINGS on restorative justice were firmly rooted in critiques of mainstream criminal justice. Restorativists were at great pains to emphasise short-comings and then, having painted a grim picture of the criminal justice landscape, would present the reader with the alternative of restorative justice—the white rabbit pulled triumphantly from the hat. Whilst section II. below explores the contested nature of defi-nitions of restorative justice, it might be helpful before we go any further to provide a brief description of restorative justice for the uninitiated reader.

Although a universal definition of restorative justice remains elusive, probably the most frequently quoted definition is provided by Tony Marshall, who sees it as

> a process whereby all the parties with a stake in a particular offence come together to resolve collectively how to deal with the aftermath of the offence and its implication for the future.[1]

An alternative (though not too dissimilar) definition is provided by Paul McCold and Ted Wachtel, who describe restorative justice

---

[1] T Marshall 'The Evolution of Restorative Justice in Britain' (1996) 4 (4) *European Journal on Criminal Policy Research*, 21, 37. Notwithstanding that it is often quoted, Marshall's definition has been widely criticised (eg, over its failure to specify the aims and outcomes of the process; who the stakeholders should be; and the nature of stakeholder participation): see, eg, J Dignan, *Understanding Victims and Restorative Justice* (Maidenhead, Open University Press, 2005) 2–5.

as a process where those primarily affected by an incident of wrong-doing come together to share their feelings, describe how they were affected and develop a plan to repair the harm done or prevent reoccurrence.[2]

They add that the essence of restorative justice 'is a collaborative problem-solving approach to social discipline intended to reintegrate individuals and repair affected communities'.[3]

What is clear from these definitions is the inclusive and collaborative nature of restorative justice's problem-solving focus, and that for an intervention to be considered to be restorative the parties have to come together in dialogue as they do in restorative conferencing and direct mediation. Further, that the restorative justice process reaches beyond victims and offenders by encompassing other stakeholders, including the wider community affected by crimes. Hence, restorative justice can be contrasted with criminal justice, even though restorative justice practices are typically situated within criminal justice *systems*.

Criminal justice refers to the statutory responses to crime and disorder of organisations such as the police, prosecutors, defence lawyers, the courts, the prisons, and probation and management offender agencies. It draws on a set of normative and theoretical justifications for attempting to limit and control the actions of citizens and, in those cases where citizens transgress, for sanctioning their behaviour and causing them pain. Such justifications fall into backward- and forward-looking aims. Forward-looking philosophies include deterrence (trying to persuade people not to reoffend), incapacitation (physically preventing them from reoffending) and rehabilitation (using education or therapy to change people's attitudes and behaviour to stop them reoffending). However, when restorative justice is compared to criminal justice, most commentators have in mind the backward-looking justifica-

---

[2] P McCold and T Wachtel, 'Restorative justice theory validation' in E Weitekamp and H-J Kerner (eds), *Restorative Justice: Theoretical Foundations* (Devon, Willan Publishing, 2002) 113.
[3] *Ibid.*

tion of retribution. Retributive justice responds to the offence committed, rather than trying to prevent further offending. It treats all citizens as moral actors who are responsible for their behaviour. Hence, it aims to punish transgressions rather than heal the transgressor, although only with as much punishment as fits the crime. In other words, the punishment must be proportionate to the crime. Retributive justice focuses on the offender and pays little regard to victims or to the wider community. Clearly, restorative justice is a distinct sentencing practice (more like mediation than other sentences such as prison or probation) and is driven by a philosophy distinct from other justifications for punishment, particularly retribution.

Restorative justice, its early advocates argued, provides a new lens through which to see crime and identify the appropriate and just responses to it. These early treatises were aspirational, even evangelistic, but rather unsophisticated.[4] In promoting the benefits of restorative justice they found it necessary to reject outright criminal justice and, in order to justify this rejection, to present it as little more than victim-insensitive, state-sponsored vengeance. Failing to acknowledge the various victim-centred and reparative measures that were already being introduced into the criminal justice system, they presented restorative and retributive justice in dichotomous terms, with the former representing all that was good about community responses to crime and the latter all that was harmful with the state monopoly over justice. Restorative justice was promoted as the answer to society's criminal ills, with its promise to bring together victims, offenders and their communities, whilst keeping the state at arm's length.

Whilst praising inclusive restorative approaches, the early literature, with few exceptions, failed to problematise concepts such as 'victim', 'offender' or 'community'. Victims and offenders were

---

[4] For a critique of evangelism in the early restorative justice literature, see J Pratt, 'Beyond Evangelical Criminology: The Meaning and Significance of Restorative Justice' in I Aertsen, T Daems and L Roberts (eds), *Institutionalizing Restorative Justice* (Cullompton, Willan, 2006).

presented as homogeneous groups, 'communities' were presumed to be supportive and inclusive, or at the very least benign, with 'society' seen as largely irrelevant. Criminal justice was criticised for having too much regard for society and too little for victims or communities, as if the latter groups were not part of wider society. All in all, concepts were blurred or undefined and the new lens had a distinctly rosy hue. This is not to say that the new product did not deserve promotion, rather that it was worthy of, and could stand up to, depiction and analysis that had integrity.

This essay makes the case for restorative justice. It argues that restorative justice can and should have a role to play in responding to most crimes and incivilities in most jurisdictions. But it does so without reliance on false dichotomies and without erecting straw men. It is unhelpful in seeking to understand the potential of restorative justice to start with the question of what is wrong with criminal justice, as so many academic commentators have. Rather, we should start with the question of what harms befall society when some of its members commit offences or behave in uncivil ways towards one other. We should not be constrained by official categories of 'victims', 'offenders' and 'crimes', but should consider *harms* done to *citizens* by criminality or antisocial behaviour. And we should then explore the various ways in which society can respond to repair those harms and to restore order, and what role restorative approaches can have in that response.

Thinking about harms in this way reveals the potential of both restorative and criminal justice, and the scope for complementary approaches that draw on both. This, of course, requires careful consideration of the potential and the limitations of both restorative and criminal justice but rejects the presumption that we should choose between the two. This essay presents arguments both for the exclusive use of restorative justice for many non-serious offences and for approaches that integrate restorative and retributive philosophies and thereby provide the scope for taking restorative practices into the 'deep end' of criminal justice (see section VI. for an explanation of the 'deep end' and 'shallow end' of criminal justice). Indeed, it is explicitly critical of the current reluctance to use restorative processes in anything but the 'shallow end' of criminal justice, most notably for young offenders or for minor offences. Hence, it considers the potential, and dangers, of restorative practices in the broader societal response to two 'deep end' crimes that test the efficacy of criminal justice: domestic violence and crimes against humanity.

In presenting the case for restorative justice, this essay adopts a clear normative stance that communities and the state in late modern society should be more restorative in responding to the harms caused by crimes, antisocial behaviours and other incivilities. It does not make a plea for a return to some romanticised notion of traditional community justice. And its pro-restorative position is not premised on the belief that the state has no appropriate role in responding to conflicts in different communities, no matter how divided or alienated those communities might be. Furthermore, it is cognisant of the dangers posed by more participatory and dialogic approaches to crimes.

What follows primarily draws on theories and philosophies of justice, rather than on empirical research. This is not because empirical research on restorative justice is without value but because it is ultimately inadequate to the task of establishing a normative position. Furthermore, some of the research on restorative justice is built on a false premise—that it is meaningful to compare restorative conferences with courts in order to evaluate the relative efficacy of both. Such comparative work is not useless—indeed, it provides valuable information on the differences and similarities between both processes, and it measures programme integrity and the extent to which restorative goals are realised in practice—however, it cannot provide proof that restorative justice is superior to criminal justice, or vice versa. This is because in asking questions about the participation of victims and offenders in the process, and the response of offenders to the process, it compares the proverbial apples with oranges. At least some of the questions which lead to the apparently greater satisfaction of both victims and offenders with restorative processes are heavily biased in its favour: questions such as 'Did you receive an apology?', 'Did you feel that the apology was sincere?', 'Did the offender understand the harm caused to you?', 'Did people indicate that you were forgiven?' are much more likely to be answered in the affirmative by those who experience restorative justice than by those who go to court. This is simply because these are the primary goals of restorative justice, but not of the court process. Whilst rarely drawing on the evidence about restorative justice in practice, this essay acknowledges up front that restorative justice often fails to live up to its potential; that there is, as in all areas of criminal justice, oftentimes a gap between justice in books and justice in action. Programme integrity is sometimes compromised, and organisational resources and sometimes apathy can conspire against the appropriate use of restorative principles in the real world. Nonetheless, given that the administration of justice can be attended to, there is value in considering the potential of restorative justice theory.

II. A ROUTE THROUGH DEFINITIONAL CONSTRAINTS AND IMPRECISION

A. Introduction

This section challenges some of the definitions used in the literature on restorative and criminal justice which limit our imagination and understanding of the two forms of justice and the relationship between them, as well as their potential to tackle harms caused by crime and disorder.

In the absence of a universally agreed definition of 'restorative justice', the concept has become deeply contested amongst its proponents and critics. Most restorative theoretical frameworks, including my own, encompass values, aims and processes that have as their common factor attempts to repair the harm caused by criminal or other types of antisocial behaviour. Restoration should address emotional as well as material loss, safety, damaged relationships, and the dignity and self-respect of victims and other stakeholders recognised as having a legitimate interest in determining the societal response to those offences committed against them. Accordingly, restorative justice is concerned with ensuring appropriate reparation to victims and their communities. But it is also aimed at lessening the fear of crime, strengthening the sense of community, and restoring the dignity of all of those harmed, including the perpetrators.

The two most frequently discussed examples of restorative justice within the extant literature are victim–offender mediation and restorative or family group conferences. These practices typically involve a face-to-face meeting between the victim and offender (or those involved in conflict where disputants cannot be categorised as such) in a safe environment to discuss the incident, the harms it has caused and how these harms should be repaired. Conferences, unlike victim–offender mediation, typically include supporters of the disputants and other concerned community members, and sometimes representatives of the state, such as police officers, social workers or housing officers. Restorative meetings can also be facilitated through indirect or 'shuttle' mediation; victims and offenders discuss their case individually with a restorative facilitator, who then feeds information back to the other party.

In face-to-face encounters, facilitators usually arrange for all those affected by an offence or an incident to attend a meeting. At the start of the meeting he or she will make clear that discussion should concentrate on the offender's *behaviour*, not its author—thus promoting the notion that the criminal act is to be condemned rather than the actor as a person. It is also made clear that the conference will ultimately focus on how the harm caused by the offence might be repaired.

Participants are helped to tell their stories by specific (often scripted) questions; to talk openly about the offence and ask relevant questions of the others, with everyone getting a chance to respond to what other people have said. The dialogic process typically begins by focusing on the perpetrator's accountability for the crime or incident. The facilitator then encourages those harmed by the incident to describe its impact, at the time and since, with a view to exploring the relationship between actions and consequences, and encouraging the perpetrator to take full responsibility for those harms. The meetings should be empowering and inclusive, and enable all stakeholders to reveal fully how the incident has affected them, with no one silenced by domination.

The facilitator's questions and prompts do not simply aim to promote communication between the participants but rather seek to encourage *constructive* dialogue. Restorative processes should address a range of damaged relationships: not only between victims and offenders, but also between offenders and their communities, and with society as a whole. Where this is realised, the prospects of the participants achieving restorative outcomes— whether an apology or material reparation—are much improved. Offenders should also be encouraged to learn from the process, in order to address those factors which may have contributed to their offending in the first place. Where the offender needs help to overcome those factors, the state should provide it, as is consistent with its duty to promote social integration.

B. Defining Victims and Offenders

The decision to prosecute offenders in eighteenth century England was generally taken by the victims, or by those they chose to represent them. Representatives of central government were only rarely involved in arbitration. There were inequities within this system, but it was clearly focussed on the resolution of conflicts and reparation of harms caused by offences.

The following two centuries witnessed the emergence and entrenchment of a professional, state-run criminal justice system. This brought about a shift from crime control mechanisms which were essentially local, personal and entrepreneurial to crime control institutions which are bureaucratic, largely impersonal and increasingly centralised. Beneath the details, the place of the victim in the design of each adversarial contest remained constant throughout this period. In all but a handful of private prosecutions—events so rare as to warrant extensive media attention when they do occur—the state, in the shape of the police and prosecutors, has become the intermediary between the victim and the court. Some sociologists, such as Nils Christie, have criticised the state for taking ownership of offences and disputes which at one time were the preserve of local individuals and communities, and in doing so usurping the right of victims to have a say in the response to their criminalisation and to seek reparation and recompense for harms suffered.[5]

This criticism was not unique to particular jurisdictions, but was at its most obvious in common law systems. In the UK and US, for example, until the changes brought about in recent decades, the role of victims had been relegated to that of witnesses, and they had been excluded from meaningful participation and decision making. This marginalisation of victims left them increasingly dissatisfied and reluctant to cooperate with the criminal justice system, as was evidenced by numerous academic and government surveys. Towards the end of the 1980s, there was mounting criticism within both the academy and victim support organisations of the treatment of victims by all criminal justice agencies. The stage was set for a further significant shift in the relationship between the state and victims.

From the late 1980s, victims' rights groups sought to enhance the place of victims in the criminal process and began to advocate that specific legal rules be introduced to give greater weight to victims' interests, and to provide them with restitution and compensation. Victims already had greater rights of participation in criminal trials in the civil law systems of Continental Europe, but political leaders elsewhere responded swiftly to the new victim awareness, and the demands of victims' groups soon found a legislative response in common law countries. This was most apparent in the introduction of measures to provide victims with information on 'their' cases, to allow victims to make personal impact statements and, in some jurisdictions, for some cases, the emergence of

---

[5] N Christie 'Conflicts as Property' (1978) 17(1) *British Journal of Criminology* 1–15.

restorative justice.[6] These reforms were introduced with the explicit aim of ensuring that the victim was no longer the forgotten actor in the criminal process and, perhaps, the less explicit aim of making sentencing more punitive.

These changes embedded within the criminal justice lexicon, as well as the public imagination, a fixed definitional and increasingly value-laden concept of victimhood. Victims' rights organisations, in particular in the US, used 'the victim' as a worthy cause to press not only for enhanced victim rights, but also for more punitive responses to offenders. With the rising power of the worthy and blameless victim in need of protection came, inevitably, diminishing respect and tolerance of those labelled as culpable dangerous offenders. The fear that such offenders were posing ever-increasing risks to society was used to justify progressively harsher and more exclusive treatment by the state. Despite persuasive empirical evidence of the significant overlap between the two groups (victims and offenders), in political rhetoric they remained distinct within a 'zero-sum' logic that saw the granting of due process protections to offenders as a denial of justice for victims.

Restorative justice does not avoid these labels. Indeed, unlike civil mediation, it is essential to restorative principles that it is made clear who is the person harmed and who has caused that harm. Furthermore, the offender is made accountable for the harms he or she has caused. However, restorative justice is about moving beyond these labels in two steps. First, once offenders have been encouraged to account for their behaviour, the process moves towards exploring the multiple layers of harms done by the offending behaviour, including harms to offenders and their supporters. Secondly, the latter part of the process shifts towards reintegrating offenders, moving on to see them as no longer distinct from the wider group. Hence, restorative justice has the potential to break down the barriers between victims and offenders and consider

---

[6] Various European countries also established institutions, legal frameworks and policies aimed at providing redress, justice and restitution to victims of crime, although—within these civil law systems—this did not require a paradigm shift in notions of justice.

instead the wider harms caused by criminal, or other damaging behaviours. It gets closer than criminal justice to seeing us all as citizens affected in various ways by harms within society.

C. Crimes and Harms

Despite falling crime rates across the US and UK, political desire to manipulate and exploit public anxieties about crime and disorder appears to be greater than ever. In the UK during the twentieth century criminal justice legislation was infrequent, but when the Labour Party were in power between 1997 and 2010 there were more than 40 crime-related Acts of Parliament, introducing changes to the criminal justice system and the creation of over 3,000 new criminal offences. This legislative hyperactivity[7] further ingrained in the public consciousness the notion of offenders as 'dangerous others', and has done little or nothing to tackle the myriad other harms suffered by citizens, including the damage done to offenders by the criminal justice system, especially prison.

The work of the social scientist Paddy Hillyard and his colleagues[8] reminds us of the wider harms that criminal justice has tended to disregard or underplay. These include harms committed by the state or corporations, and non-criminal—and sometimes more serious—harms, such as unemployment, pollution or poverty. The criminal justice process, they point out, devotes considerable attention and resources to many quite trivial behaviours or events where the harms endured by victims, if there are any, are

[7] I Loader 'Ice cream and incarceration: On appetites for security and punishment' (2009)11(2) *Punishment & Society*, 241–257.

[8] P Hillyard, C Pantazis, S Tombs and D Gordon, *Beyond Criminology: Taking Harm Seriously* (London, Pluto Press, 2004); P Hillyard and S Tombs, 'From "crime" to social harm?' (2007) 48 *Crime, Law and Social Change* 9. Hillyard *et al* aim to develop a new academic discipline, called 'Zemiology' (from the Greek *zemia*, which translates as 'harm' or 'damage' or 'loss'), focused on the range of social harms which people experience throughout their lives, only a small proportion of which fall under the remit of the criminal law.

minimal. By focusing on harms rather than crimes, the authors look critically at the damage done to individuals caught up in the criminal justice system, pointing out that it often outweighs the harms caused by the original crime.

However, even if we recognise pain caused by the criminal process, in particular by prison, it is not necessary to adopt an abolitionist stance, as Hillyard does. Neither is it necessary to dismiss the values embodied by the criminal law. Those acts which are criminalised are, by and large, not only harmful but immoral, in that they are perpetrated by those who intend to do harm, or at least are reckless to the probable consequences of their actions. In other words, we have to consider 'wrongs' as well as 'harms'. However, Hillyard's thesis is helpful in exploring harms beyond criminal acts and the damage caused by the criminal justice system, and in alerting us to the costs of penal excess. Furthermore, it focuses our attention on the sometimes myopic approach of criminal justice in its failure adequately to acknowledge the context within which people commit offences. It helps us to acknowledge that, given wider social injustices, not all offenders are equally culpable. Moreover, it reminds us that whilst criminal justice envisages a contest between the offender and the state, it generally fails to recognise or respond to harms caused to the wider community.

While restorative justice is about holding offenders accountable for their behaviour, it allows for consideration of the wider responsibilities of others in their community and the state. It does not seek to apportion blame to the offender's family or friends, but puts the offence (or other harmful behaviour) in the context of relative deprivation, dysfunctional relationships, poor educational or health services, or failures of those in authority to identify or respond effectively to evident criminogenic factors. Recognition and discussion of these contexts allows participants in the restorative process to see beyond the label 'offender' to a sometimes confused and vulnerable person who may have been harmed by his or her experiences as much as he or she has harmed others. As such, restorative processes can break down negative preconceptions about those who offend and provide instead a space for sympathy, and sometimes empathy.

Of course mitigation evidence presented in a criminal court is supposed to do the same, and yet it often fails to bridge the empathic divide[9] between the 'respectable' jury and the 'disrespectful' offender in the dock. This is partly because the evidence is provided by criminal justice professionals and is seen as part of an adversarial process whereby both sides do their best to win their case. Information given by parents, teachers or friends of the offender on the context within which harms have been done is more likely to be persuasive in making sense of transgressions. What is more, information provided by the offender, with the chance for other participants to seek clarification or to ask for further information, is most likely to reveal the multi-faceted nature of the offender and the offence. In other words, restorative justice has greater potential to close the social distance between victims and offenders, to bridge the empathic divide and create the context in which all participants are seen as citizens worthy of consideration and respect, as well as revealing *all* of the harms caused by the offending behaviour and consequent reactions.

Harms to those beyond the people labelled 'victims' are much more likely to be disclosed in a restorative conference than in a court. Whilst only legal witnesses to the offence have the opportunity to give evidence to a court, and then only in those cases where the defendant pleads 'not guilty' and their evidence is required, anyone considered to be harmed by the offence should have the opportunity to contribute to a restorative meeting. Restorative justice therefore reveals the multiple and diverse harms caused by offending or harmful behaviours, including, of course, to the offender. But what do we mean by 'restorative justice'?

---

[9] An 'empathic divide' is a cognitive and emotional distance between one group or one person and another (eg a jury and a defendant) that acts as a psychological barrier to genuine understanding and insight. See C Haney, *Death by Design: Capital Punishment as a Social Psychological System* (Oxford, Oxford University Press, 2005) 203.

D. Restorative Justice and Restorative Practices

Whilst some restorativists have focused on developing a theory of restorative justice, others have attempted to define restorative justice by practices, describing as 'restorative' any new initiative that does not follow the typical trajectory of arrest, prosecution, conviction and punishment. The development of a clear understanding of restorative justice is frustrated by this confusing application of the label to a variety of often disparate practices, including the provision of services (for example, victim support services), certain procedural reforms (for example, victim impact statements) and various court-imposed sanctions (such as community service and victim compensation orders).

It may help the reader in considering both the potential and the pitfalls of restorative justice to find a way past this definitional imprecision, and that might be facilitated by establishing a conceptual distinction between 'restorative justice' and 'restorative practices'. Restorative *justice* is best conceived of as a relatively narrow concept that requires dialogue between the offender and the victim, although this does not have to be face-to-face but can be a type of 'shuttle mediation'. Dialogic processes refer, at the most basic level, to processes where people engage in dialogue with each other. This is different from the 'monologues' typically heard in criminal courts, where defence and prosecution lawyers talk at adjudicators (judges, magistrates and juries), and where those people most affected by criminal behaviour (victims and offenders) rarely talk at all, and certainly not to each other. Dialogic processes are dynamic and relational, with individual actors sometimes modifying their narratives in response to others' accounts. Unlike dialectical processes, they are not logical investigations aimed at one unequivocal truth. Dialogic processes do not require a synthesis of competing narratives or that one actor subjugate another's account.

Restorative measures such as victim support, victim impact statements and judicially-imposed reparative measures (for example, community service and compensation orders) are not dialogic, although they are motivated by certain restorative aims, such as the restoration of a sense of safety within a community. They have at their heart an attempt to recognise the unique status of the victim, who had, until the last decade or so, become increasingly marginalised in modern, purely retributive justice common law systems. They are more helpfully defined as restorative *practices*. This distinction works at the level of everyday 'domestic' criminality. For example, a victim impact statement made by someone who has been burgled allows for victim participation and, controversially, might bring about victim influence on sentencing, but it does not provide a mechanism for victim–offender dialogue.

The distinction maintains itself in the deep end of criminal justice. For example, in the domain of crimes against humanity, *gacaca* courts in Rwanda perhaps come closest to implementing restorative justice, as they bring together victims, offenders and the wider community to discuss the harms caused by acts committed during the genocide of April 1994. However, *gacaca* has introduced restorative practices rather than pure restorative justice into Rwanda. Indeed, it is better understood as a hybrid system in which restorative encounters are mediated through fixed legal boundaries, with processes resulting in both reparative community-based sentences and retributive sentences, including a return to prison.[10] *Gacaca* and other transitional justice mechanisms—such as truth and reconciliation commissions that are referred to by many as restorative justice—are more usefully understood as restorative *practices*. This essay primarily focuses on restorative justice; on processes aimed at bringing together victims, offenders and their communities in meaningful dialogue aimed at repairing the harms done, although it discusses restorative practices and criminal justice where applicable.

---

[10] P Clark, 'Hybridity, Holism, and "Traditional" justice: the case of the *Gacaca* courts in post-genocide Rwanda' (2007) 39 *The George Washington International Law Review* 765.

III. COMMUNITY AT THE HEART OF
RESTORATIVE JUSTICE

In many diagrammatic descriptions of restorative justice the reader is presented with a triangle to represent the three main parties harmed by crime and therefore included in restorative encounters: the victims, the offenders, and the community. Given the significance of community, it is worth spending some time to reflect on this concept. This is not the place to survey the use of the term in the sociological literature on restorative justice, or to attempt an authoritative definition of what 'community' means, but rather to say a little about how the concept is operationalised in restorative encounters.

Years of sociological contemplation of the concept of community have failed to pin it down. Community is often used to describe a group of people organised around shared beliefs, values and norms. The group is bigger than a mere family unit but has traditionally been conceived of as smaller than a nation.[11] Traditionally the concept of community was restrained by geography, with local areas (neighbourhoods, villages or even gated housing estates) providing communities of location. Increased mobility and more transient populations generally have challenged the salience of geography, so that people today can be part of multiple communities—kinship, friendship and professional—regardless of where they live. Furthermore, communities are no longer bound by face-to-face communication: communities of people with shared lifestyles, interests or professional connections who are geographically dispersed can communicate regularly through the Internet. Indeed, some academics have more intellectual discourse within their virtual communities than with their colleagues in neighbouring offices. Other communities for whom geography is irrelevant are established around identity: ethnic, religious or disability, for example.

---

[11] More recent popular use of the term has, however, extended to refer to like-minded people across the world; witness the emergence of the phrase 'global' or 'international' community.

Communities are not mutually exclusive but are often integrated and nested. Most of us belong to more than one community and are close to people who we can easily fit into two or more of our significant communities. Hence, in preparing for a restorative intervention, facilitators need to identify the most appropriate 'community' to include. This is partly dependent on the crime and partly dependent on the offender and victim. Whilst courts' jury-selection methods are aimed at recruiting a neutral cross-sample of society to judge offenders and exclude anyone known to the offender or victim or directly harmed by the offence, the converse is true for restorative justice. Facilitators of restorative processes try to recruit relevant communities—people who have significant relationships with one or more of the participants, or who have been affected by the offence. They are included because they can provide a community of support to the main actors—the victims and offenders—and because they have also been harmed by the offence or they represent people who have been harmed by the offence. In this sense, whilst they are not direct victims, they could be seen as indirect or secondary victims. They may, for example, be residents in a neighbourhood where the offender has damaged public property, or they may be teachers in a school where pupils have been hurt. They are not neutral, objective adjudicators, as jurors are supposed to be, but have a pre-existing connection to the offender, the victim or the offence that is seen as bestowing on them certain rights or obligations to participate in the response to the offence.

There is often a gap between theory and practice in operational-ising the concept of community in restorative justice. It is easy to identify a geographical community when the offence has been committed within a residential area. For example, graffiti on the walls of a village hall or criminal damage to a playground damage the fabric of that community and the feelings of safety of those who live in the vicinity, any of whom may be appropriate for inclusion in a restorative session. It is less obvious who might be identified as the harmed community when the graffiti are on a motorway bridge or in an underground train station. For other offences communities are relatively easy to identify but less easy to include, communities of identity being the obvious example. Violence against homosexuals because they are homosexuals (offences typically labelled as 'hate crimes') can, if widely reported, affect that community as well as the individual victims. They act as a reminder of a wider hate or prejudice, and they can raise the fear of crime amongst that population. However, it is not necessarily easy for a facilitator to identify and invite other homosexuals to participate in a restorative encounter, unless they choose to invite representatives from a gay rights organisation, for example. Only those restorative measures established with the explicit aim of responding to crimes against a community, such as truth and reconciliation processes, regularly achieve meaningful community integration in the process. For this reason, most restorative processes involve communities around the victims and perpetrators rather than the offence. In this sense, they involve 'communities of concern', whose concern is with the victim or offender and only tangentially with the offence.

Domestic violence provides an example of an overlap between concern about the key participants and concern about the offence. Even when violence in the home is directed only at one individual, for example a wife, it will impact on the whole family. Not only children, but also adult siblings, grandparents and others will be affected by fear, anger and frustration, emotions that might well be further complicated by familial obligations or divided loyalties. They may wish to contribute to a restorative intervention both to share their experiences and to receive support from significant others. And they may wish to support either or both the victim and perpetrator; people towards whom they have, by nature of their shared community, an established commitment, even if they do not share the same values or expectations about relationships.

In the sociological literature, community means a commitment to shared norms and values, from which emerges a shared identity or culture. But communities in restorative justice need to be more than just groups of individuals with shared interests, motivated only by addressing their own concerns with others who think like them or who can serve their needs; they need to be those who have some responsibility towards one another and a commitment to attend to each others' needs. In this sense, community in restorative justice is more akin to the concept of *Gemeinschaft* than *Gesellschaft*. The German sociologist, Ferdinand Tönnies, introduced these categories to describe two distinct forms of human association in the late nineteenth century, but they have become relatively common phases used within and beyond the academy.[12] *Gemeinschaft* refers to communities where the individual members are motivated by common mores and beliefs. In contrast, *Gesellschaft* may be translated as 'civil society', where individuals are motivated by their own self-interest and do not necessarily share the same norms and values. To introduce a cliché, communities in restorative justice need to move beyond sharing to caring; caring about the offence and the harm it has done to themselves and to others, caring about the direct victim, where there is one, and caring about the offender and what now happens to him or her. In some cases victim and offender will come from the same community and the offence will have harmed that very community in some tangible way. Often, however, they will come from different communities and the offence will have little impact on anyone beyond those individuals directly involved. In the former case the restorative meeting is aimed at repairing the harms done to that community, with the ultimate aim of reintegrating the offender back into the community. In the latter case something different can happen: new communities (around the offence) can be established. These are mostly temporary in order to deal effectively with the aftermath of the offence and to provide restoration for the parties involved, but occasionally may become permanent, if circumstances allow.

The work of Morgan Scott Peck may be helpful in exploring how this can happen, how it is that strangers, already alienated from one another by the actions of an offender, can establish a community,

---

[12] F Tönnies, *Gemeinscaft und Gesellschaft* (1887), English translation *Community and Society: Gemeinschaft und Gesellschaft* by CP Loomis (Michigan, The Michigan State University Press, 1957).

and how those previously known to one another can re-establish their community after it has been damaged by the transgressions of one of their own. Best known for his work on human fulfilment,[13] Scott Peck set out in *The Different Drum*[14] what he believed to be the salient features of a 'true community': notably, inclusivity, commitment and consensus; realism; contemplation; a safe place; a laboratory for personal disarmament; a group that can fight gracefully; a group of all leaders; and a spirit. He envisaged a community that can celebrate individuality and transcend differences, and can share vulnerabilities and make a commitment to resolving conflicts, healing and peacemaking with mutual respect, compassion and understanding, without losing an appreciation of the world outside. He argued that communities do not always emerge organically but can be consciously built. Whilst his focus was on the establishment of new communities, his description of the stages that can bring about functioning communities has resonance for restorative conferencing for strangers and for those pre-existing communities that have been damaged by crime and are in need of restoration. He identifies four stages of community-building: pseudo-community; chaos; emptiness; and true community.

In the first stage, pseudo-community, Scott Peck describes participants 'playing nice' with one another, hiding their differences and grievances, and showing only their most agreeable sides. He argues that movement on from this stage needs to be facilitated fairly quickly in order that true community can emerge. For those of us who have observed restorative conferences, this stage is all too familiar. Whilst occasionally conferences start with angry confrontation, more often than not they begin with polite exchanges, with formality and disguise, with introductions but not revelations. Even those participants already known to one another are usually quite reserved at this stage. It takes a strong facilitator and challenging questions to encourage shy and nervous participants to

[13] M Scott Peck, *The Road Less Travelled: A New Psychology of Love, Traditional Values and Spiritual Growth* (New York, Simon and Schuster, 1978).

[14] M Scott Peck, *The Different Drum: Community Making and Peace* (New York, Simon and Schuster, 1987).

reveal how they have felt and still feel about what they or others have done. In most restorative conferencing schemes the offenders are asked to describe their thoughts and feelings at the time of the offence and subsequently. The other participants are then invited to talk about the harm the offence caused. It is at this stage that the conference typically moves to something similar to Scott Peck's 'chaos' stage.

By chaos, Scott Peck envisaged the stage at which participants move to a more authentic and honest discussion of how they feel and what they believe. At this stage they are able to open up, rather than being constrained by a desire to cooperate. He saw this as an essential step towards true community. In restorative conferences it is vital that participants are able to challenge not only the behaviours of others, but also their own justifications and rationales. Some offenders indulge in what sociologists have referred to as 'techniques of neutralisation'[15]—attempts to blame others, excuse themselves, or minimise the harms they have done—because to take full responsibility is uncomfortable or even painful. In the chaos stage others might try to resist this, sometimes quite forcefully, in order that the offender is held fully accountable for his or her actions. Of course, it is not only the dispute between victims and offenders that is open to discussion; sometimes unresolved or even previously unacknowledged tensions between other members of the community are thrown into the pot. For example, parents of young offenders sometimes raise concerns about their child's other (non-criminal) behaviours, and use the forum to try to resolve differences in beliefs about how the family should live together and, in particular, about how the child should conduct himself or herself. Youths, in turn, might take the opportunity to reveal resentments about their parents' handling of them; their perceptions of neglect or inequities in treatment amongst siblings. As Scott Peck noted about this stage, these revelations, accusations and counter-accusations, whilst essential for clearing the air, put an

---

[15] G M Sykes and D Matza, 'Techniques of Neutralisation: A Theory of Delinquency' (1957) XXII *American Sociological Review* 664.

enormous burden on the facilitator, who needs to provide a safe space for honest debate whilst protecting participants from denigration. Skilled facilitation and clear rules of engagement can help to bring about civil dialogue and redress transgressions when they occur.

At first glance, Scott Peck's third stage towards true community seems to be counter-intuitive. For him, 'emptiness' is the stage where the participants have stopped trying to persuade each other of their own perspective and are able to acknowledge others' wounds. It is at this stage in a restorative conference that a meaningful apology is most likely. Offenders sometimes offer an apology to their victims and other members of the conference early on, when describing what they did. However, apology in the absence of reflection on the harms done more often than not rings hollow. For apologies to be meaningful to victims they must come from an offender who fully acknowledges both his guilt and the legitimacy of the law he has broken. Victims in particular want to know that the offender fully understands the harms he or she has done to them and to the wider community, and fully accepts that he or she is accountable for those harms before offering an apology. In other words, victims want 'informed apologies'. Sometimes, given the revelations of the 'chaos stage', others find reasons to apologise too; sometimes to the victim, if it is thought that some failed to protect him or her from the harms, and sometimes to the offender, who may have been let down by family or friends in the past. Victims can also find reasons to forgive the offender, recognising that those who have damaged them, their property or feelings of security, have themselves been damaged by others, although facilitators and other participants should not expect or require the victim to forgive the offender, as this would put unreasonable pressure on those most harmed by offences.

The final stage—true community—is brought about by the previous revelations and responses, and is characterised by empathy, understanding and compassion. It is during this stage that a reparation agreement can be finalised. Understanding the impact of their behaviour leads some offenders to make reparative gestures to build on the apologies offered in the previous stage. Sometimes an offender pitches his reparation offer too high or too low for the other participants, but empathy, tolerance and compassion for both the offender and victim built up among the other participants during the conference can help in the negotiation of over-generous or disproportionately low offers of reparation. Participants who have been through the previous stages have the confidence to challenge one another in a respectful but assertive way. When the restorative conference comes to an end, visual displays of compassion and the bridging of divides, such as hugs, smiles or handshakes, are not uncommon. Empathetic exchanges about the difficulties experienced by participants during this conference and other shared experiences further secure developing bonds and leave the participants in successful conferences part of a new community of concern, and the participants from previously established communities reintegrated.

This is not the place to critique Scott Peck's recipe for community-building but rather to use it as an heuristic device for describing the dynamics of restorative meetings and for understanding why restorative justice can help in the establishment and maintenance of community when that very community might be thought to be at its most vulnerable. Community encompasses values such as commitment to others, mutuality, respect and trust (core values of restorative justice), and it is not coincidental that sociological interest in not only describing community but identifying measures to create and sustain community has arisen at a time of increasing fragmentation and diversity, when geography no longer binds us to significant others.

The values of a community are threatened, and can be broken, by transgressions, in particular crime. When somebody commits a criminal offence he or she offends not only against the laws of the country or state, but also against the norms and values of his or her community. Hence, families, friends, colleagues and others can feel not only disappointed in the behaviour of the offender, but also that the behaviour has challenged their own sense of security and stability. By breaking the bonds of their communities, offenders might exclude themselves, or be excluded by others, from that community. These bonds (especially mutual commitment and trust) need to be re-established if the offenders are to be reintegrated into, and derive benefits from, their communities. Before reintegration, however, the community needs to, and importantly has a right to, censure those who have transgressed community norms in order to reassert social order and shared commitment to the norms. Advocates of restorative processes argue that conferences are better able to achieve this than criminal courts. This is in large part because they facilitate interaction and enhance social capital, and can even provide it for some whose lives have previously been bereft of networks of trust and reciprocity. In this sense, restorative conferences are better able than other criminal justice processes to integrate or reintegrate offenders.

However, in some cases communities need to do more than just open their arms and reintegrate; they need to resocialise the offender. Offenders who have been excluded, or who have excluded themselves, from law-abiding communities, and who become enmeshed in anti-social gangs characterised by defiance or rejection of mainstream norms and values, will need to be resocialised if they are to 'go straight'. They will need to re-learn the norms and behaviours necessary for acceptance into those communities most able to help them desist from offending. Of course, one of the attractions of using restorative practices for youths is that they are already in a process of socialisation. Childhood is the period when most formative instruction about how to behave takes place. Families, schools and communities repeatedly try to teach young people about behaviours, desires and goals that are appropriate to that community. However, socialisation does not end when adulthood begins; adults are frequently resocialised into new sets of norms or values as societies change or as their individual circumstances change. Whilst adults may not be as malleable as children, or as happy to have appropriate behaviours prescribed to them, restorative processes have the potential to resocialise them as well as juveniles.

The process of resocialisation starts with the questions asked of offenders about why they committed the offence, questions which invite consideration not only of the immediate precipitating features of the offence, but also of the criminogenic factors in their lives. However, it is most apparent in the less formal discussions that typically follow the structured, facilitator-led part of the conference. After a series of questions about motivations, experiences and harms caused, there typically comes a prompt to consider what could be done to repair the harms done. More often than not, this leads not only to a discussion about reparation to the victim, but also to a more general consideration of what changes there need to be in the offender's life in order to prevent the likelihood of his or her reoffending. These might be changes in habits, friendship groups, education or employment, or in family relationships, and they may include treatment for drug or alcohol misuse or anger management. It is during this discussion that participants articulate any discordance between the norms, values and beliefs of the group and those of the offender, and discuss how the offender might change to fit better into the wider, law-abiding community.

It is this potential to resocialise that is at the heart of enthusiasm for restorative justice. While broader restorative practices can help victims to recover from crimes, can provide material reparation to communities affected by crime and rehabilitation for offenders, only restorative justice can resocialise offenders into, or back into, law-abiding communities and encourage 'pro-social behaviour'. Pro-social behaviour is caring about the rights and welfare of others, and about acting in ways that enhance their welfare. Although rarely articulated as thus, this, it seems to me, is the main aspiration of restorative justice. It is a pity, and surprising, therefore, that there is so little restorative justice around.

IV. A REFLECTION ON THE IMBALANCE BETWEEN RESTORATIVE ASPIRATIONS AND RESTORATIVE PRACTICES

A. Restorative Justice in the UK: All Talk and Little or No Action

Over the past decade, and in particular since the start of the new millennium, there seems to have been more written and talked about restorative justice than any other criminological topic. In addition to the published work, there have been numerous national and international conferences and seminars each year held within and outside the academy, and a stream of e-conversations and debates taking place weekly on various restorative justice e-mail lists. At the same time, in the UK and beyond, numerous pieces of legislation have introduced restorative practices into the criminal justice process. Despite this, there remains little restorative activity on the ground in many jurisdictions. Indeed, restorative justice, particularly in the UK, is fast becoming the most over-evaluated and under-practised area of criminal justice. We should pause for a moment to reflect on this apparent imbalance and to consider reasons for the continued enthusiasm for restorative justice in light of relative inactivity, taking the UK as a case study, although other European jurisdictions or the US might have been used.

At present, there is a handful of restorative justice programs operating throughout the UK. For the most part, they are administered by the police or Youth Offending Teams (YOTs) and are, typically, available only for shallow-end crime. Since 1997, when 'New Labour' came to power in Britain, criminal justice legislation has been in overdrive, introducing various restorative practices, although alongside more punitive and exclusionary measures. In 1998, police cautions for young offenders were replaced with 'reprimands' and 'warnings', influenced by restorative principles. Scope for restorative practices and a consultative role for victims is also provided by the power given to the courts to impose reparation orders and action plan orders on young offenders.

Since 1999 there has been a mandatory sentence of 'referral order' to a 'Youth Offender Panel' for most young offenders pleading guilty and appearing before a youth or magistrates' court for the first time (and just recently this has been extended to second offences). A Youth Offender Panel consists of two volunteers recruited directly from the local community, alongside one member of the local YOT.[16] The panel meets with the young person, and usually his or her parents, to talk about the reasons for the offending behaviour and to explore how to put things right. Victims should be asked if they wish to attend the panel to explain how the crime affected them, and to contribute to the establishment of a reparative and rehabilitative programme for the offender and the 'contract' for its completion. Thus, the procedures followed at a panel meeting, and any activities specified in the resulting contract, should be informed by principles of restorative justice: taking responsibility for the consequences of offending behaviour; making reparation to the victim; and achieving reintegration (or integration) into the community. However, victims attend panel meetings in less than 10 per cent of cases, and research has shown that too often lay panel members are not seen by offenders as representing their communities. Indeed, lay panel members in many cases are thought to act more punitively than the (professional) YOT panel member, and to be more inclined to denigrate than reintegrate.

Adult cautions with reparative conditions attached—'conditional cautions'—were introduced in 2003. However, preliminary research suggests that very few police services are issuing restorative, conditional cautions and that almost none involve victims. Instead, they tend to be relatively informal chats between the offender and police officer, who is supposed to represent the interests of the victim as well as the wider community, although

[16] Every local authority in England and Wales has a YOT made up of representatives from the police, Probation Service, social services, health, education, drugs and alcohol misuse and housing. The YOTs identify the specific problems that make the young person offend, as well as measuring the risk they pose to others, and identify suitable programs to address the needs of the young person with the intention of preventing further offending.

almost always without actually seeking out the views of either. Since 2008, new Youth Restorative Disposals (YRDs) have been used to hold 10- to 17-year-olds to account for minor crime and disorder. Typically, a police officer, who is meant to be trained for the YRD, will act 'on the spot', if circumstances allow, and facilitate a brief meeting between the two parties. The victim has the opportunity to talk about the effect the incident had on him or her, and, according to government guidance, there *may* be an apology. A young person can receive only one YRD, and can go through the procedure only if all parties are present and consent to participate. This new intervention is currently subject to a pilot study and so there is no evidence of its use or efficacy, but research on similar initiatives suggests that these disposals may be far removed from the theory and philosophy of restorative justice.

It seems, from this brief perusal of recent legislation, that—in England and Wales at least—there is a good deal of legislation but in practice little restorative justice that brings together victims, offenders and their wider communities. Furthermore, these measures have too often found themselves upstaged by a sudden need for a shot of political adrenalin. High-profile cases, especially those involving child offenders, have been exploited to justify various control measures imposed on ever younger 'feral youths' and their 'inadequate' or 'irresponsible' parents. What do we deduce from this? Might it be that New Labour, who promised so much to those who saw through the 'prison works' mantra of the previous administration, was using restorative justice as a cynical ploy to tighten the bonds of social control—widening the net of criminal justice with the promise of restoration? If the state had hijacked the language of restoration in its drive to become more punitive and controlling, this might well explain the large and arguably increasing gap between rhetoric and action.

Almost a decade ago, speculating on the apparent contradictions in New Labour criminal justice policy in a special edition of *The Political Quarterly*,[17] my co-author and I suggested two, not

---

[17] C Hoyle and D Rose, 'Labour, Law and Order' (2001) 72(1) *Political Quarterly* 76.

necessarily exclusive, explanations. The first, rather pessimistically, pointed to the notion of conditional citizenship, with 'decent' people having rights and 'louts' having responsibilities. The second, more generous, explanation was rooted in a lack of confidence: we argued that Labour's fear of being seen to be soft on crime (having gone into an election with the notorious promise to be tough on crime and tough on its causes) spawned socially excluding and intolerant policies alongside more welfarist, restorative measures, creating this uneasy contradiction. Thus some progressive changes had been smuggled into the legislative programme by stealth, rather than proclaimed with the clarity and courage they deserved, and—partly in consequence—had not been adequately resourced. As I write this essay, some nine years later, when New Labour has ceded power to a new Conservative/Liberal Democrat government, our first explanation seems more persuasive. If we look beyond the borders of the UK, however, we find that the failure of restorative justice to become embedded in the criminal justice system is far from inevitable.

In Northern Ireland, for example, there is rather more restorative activity for youths. Since the Justice (Northern Ireland) Act 2002, youth conferences have been used for all types of offences, except those that would attract a life sentence if the offender was an adult, while offenders can receive a youth conference referral on more than one occasion. In New Zealand, since the Children, Young Persons and their Families Act 1989, about a quarter of cases—the most serious (except murder and manslaughter) and those involving repeat young offenders—have received restorative interventions, in the form of family group conferences, with the majority of cases reaching an agreement that avoids prosecution. Other cases are dealt with through warnings or diversionary plans (including restorative processes). However, New Zealand would appear to be the exception that makes the rule. Restorative conferencing is not so widespread in the US (indeed some states have little or no restorative activity), in Australia or in Europe, although there are pockets of more intense restorative activity throughout the world.

Academic studies suggest that, in addition to political ambivalence about criminal justice policy, resources and organisational goals militate against effective restorative justice in various jurisdictions. And yet governments continue to introduce restorative initiatives, the United Nations has made a clear commitment to them, and academics continue to write about them: continued enthusiasm in the face of inactivity. In particular, there seems to be an inverse relationship between justice practices and academic scrutiny. The criminal courts are in operation every working day of the year, and yet there is comparatively little academic research on how they operate and to what effect. Similarly, prosecutors and defence solicitors are continually processing cases, and yet, since Mike McConville and his colleagues published their seminal academic texts *Case for the Prosecution* and *Standing Accused* in the early 1990s,[18] in-depth studies of these highly significant legal actors in the criminal process have been thin on the ground. Meanwhile, the same period has witnessed the emergence of a vast literature on—the relatively rare—restorative conferencing. In trying to account for this apparently disproportionate academic response we get close to the essence of restorative justice—its fundamental optimism.

B. A Criminology of Hope

Part of the explanation for the disproportionate academic attention on restorative justice can be found in the novelty factor. Initially, at least, academics may have been attracted to restorative justice simply because it was not an over-populated field; not only the public, but other academics too were ignorant about its theoretical underpinnings and practices, and academics seeking research grants or publications could almost guarantee interest in their work. However, there is a more compelling and less cynical

---

[18] M McConville, A Sanders and R Leng, *The Case for the Prosecution* (London, Routledge, 1991); M McConville, J Hodgson, L Bridges and A Pavlovic, *Standing Accused: The Organization and Practices of Criminal Defence Lawyers in Britain* (Oxford, Oxford University Press, 1994).

reason for its initial attraction, and certainly for its continued hold on academic attention: it provides jaded academics, as well as jaded practitioners, with aspirations and optimism. What is more, it seems to hold the promise of a fairer and more constructive way of doing justice for some liberals and communitarians.

For liberal academics (and many sociologists and criminologists are), restorative justice runs counter to the prevailing punitive wind. It presents an alternative to the popular punitivism that has characterised criminal justice policy and practice for the past decade or so in the UK and the US, and beyond, albeit to a lesser degree. At the time of writing there are almost 85,000 people in prisons in England and Wales, and 2.3 million in the US; indeed, when we include those in jail, prison, on probation or on parole in the US, this figure jumps to approximately 7.3 million, or 1 in every 31 American adults. This represents a crisis of penal policy and sentencing. Sentencing has become more severe, with custody being used far more often than it used to be in spite of a declining crime rate in both jurisdictions, including for crimes of violence, and with no persuasive evidence that incapacitation has significantly reduced crime rates.

Governments are not only incarcerating increasing numbers of people—often young people—they have simultaneously pursued other exclusionary policies. For example, they have introduced or threatened to introduce initiatives aimed at naming and shaming and registering those considered to be beyond the boundaries of acceptability and tolerance, and excluding those who are not deemed to be responsible citizens (see the Jacob Wetterling Crimes Against Children and Sexually Violent Offender Registration Act 1994 and 'Megan's law'[19] in the US; and sex offender registers and attempts to introduce 'Sarah's law' in the UK). These, and other similar policies, provide evidence of a more general attempt to exclude 'undesirables', either through incarceration or through legislation which keeps out of the law-abiding and morally decent community those who have erred or those who offend our sensibilities. Add to this

---

[19] HR 2137, 104th Congress, Second Session (1996).

dismal landscape penalising policies for managing other 'non-citizens', such as those with insecure immigration status or those seeking asylum, and we see the emergence of postmodern societies characterised by intolerance and fear of 'the other'.

Even so-called community sentences have been made increasingly exclusionary in the current climate of fear. For example, in the UK, those who are ordered to serve sentences of unpaid work in the community are now required, by a Ministry of Justice sentencing policy, to wear bright orange reflective jackets whilst carrying out their community work. These jackets, which are emblazoned with the words 'community payback' in bold letters on the back, are, according to the Minster for Justice, about meeting the public's expectation that justice is *seen* to be done and, in that way, restoring public faith in community sentences. They are, in fact, just another attempt to humiliate and stigmatise offenders, and to ensure that they are seen to be separate from the law-abiding community, not part of it. It is no accident, for example, that they are orange: the 'chain gangs' of American prisoners required to perform menial or physically challenging work as a form of punishment either wore stripes or distinctive orange jumpsuits to make clear to the public their status as convicts. Whilst these were mostly phased out by the 1950s, more recently prisoners at the notorious US Guantánamo Bay Detention Camp were made to wear similar orange jumpsuits. To suggest that the introduction of a policy similarly to attire those serving community sentences in the UK has nothing to do with attempts to denigrate prisoners is utterly dishonest.

Contemporary exclusionary and punitive policies and rhetoric have been understood by criminologists in relation to the emergence of a 'risk society', a 'criminology of everyday life' and a 'criminology of the other'; all of which have resulted in increasing demonisation and exclusion of certain citizens for the protection of others, and in the development of policies to keep suspicious 'others' away from ourselves and our property.[20] Risk assessment

---

[20] See D Garland 'The Limits of the Sovereign State: Strategies of Crime Control in Contemporary Society' (1996) 36(4) *British Journal of Criminology* 445.

and management policies focus on public protection through the management and exclusion of menacing individuals and groups. Their focus is on separating the risky from the vulnerable, rather than attempting to resocialise those deemed to be at risk so that they can be reintegrated into safe communities. Part of a risk management approach is to make ourselves less vulnerable to those considered to be dangerous by erecting barriers, including physical barriers. In this sense, it accords with the 'criminology of everyday life', which refers to a change in social mores whereby crime has become accepted as a constant threat that must be guarded against routinely through situational crime prevention. Society, under these influences, creates physical and moral domains that are not sympathetic to, and even militate against, inclusive notions of community. They fail to challenge and may even perpetuate the 'criminology of the other' that is seen to be at the core of modern penality: the labelling of predatory offenders as 'them', considered to be distinct from the moral and law-abiding 'us'. Within a global community with high levels of legal and illegal mobility and the 'threat of the other' (immigrants, asylum seekers, criminal networks, terrorists, etc), those wishing to promote community-based, parsimonious responses to criminal infractions must row hard against the punitive tide.

If the political left is driving the exclusionary and punitive agenda, and is considered by some to be suffering from a legitimacy deficit, where can liberals turn for a challenge to this new penal orthodoxy? Some academics, dismayed by the increasingly shrill call for greater use of state-imposed sanctions and exclusions, find respite in restorative justice. It suggests to them that spiralling prison sentences are not an inevitable result of post-modernity, and that there could be an alternative, less damaging social and political response to a range of social problems and harmful behaviours, criminal and otherwise. Restorative justice attracted the attention of those outside, as well as within, the academy because it held the promise of reducing offending at a time when academics and policy makers were still reeling from the 'nothing works' response to rehabilitation. Restorative justice emerged at the same time as the 'what works' agenda,[21] and was soon imbued with expectations of its efficacy. With two out of three people, and three-quarters of all young offenders, reoffending within two years of release from prison, it was already clear that as an instrument of desistance (the cessation of offending) our prisons were as ineffective as ever. But little was known about restorative justice, and some academics and practitioners made it their goal to show that this apparently less punitive and less exclusionary way of responding to offenders might benefit society at large by reducing crime.

More than this, though, they explored the potential of restorative justice to provide a fairer and more decent way of responding to crime. Involvement of victims had been the vogue for over a decade, but unlike other inclusive schemes, restorative justice did not seem to be about using victims to make sentences harsher. It gave all those harmed by offences a legitimate role to play and treated them with dignity and respect. It seemed to have the potential to make criminal justice and society more generally a better, more civilised place, and it was this potential that was grasped at by world-weary liberals tired of denigrative and exclusionary policies. And despite limited restorative activity and limited evidence of the efficacy of restorative processes, academics continue to write of the promise of restorative justice.

C. Appeals to Communitarianism

As mentioned above, in the UK the language of restorative justice gained currency in Tony Blair's New Labour Government, which made clear its intention of making a break with 18 years of Conservative policies on law and order. In particular, restorative

---

[21] Government 'what works' initiatives were aimed at reducing re-offending by ensuring that all work done with offenders was based on empirical evidence of success, evidence typically provided by criminologists or government researchers who evaluated programmes and interventions in order to help probation services to deliver effective, well-designed programmes to those on whom they were likely to have an impact. See F T Cullen and P Gendreau, 'From nothing works to what works: Changing professional ideology in the 21st century' (2001) 81 *The Prison Journal* 313.

justice can be seen there—in part at least—as a reaction to the libertarian rejection of the notion of society that characterised Margaret Thatcher's administration, if not so much that of her successor, John Major. Like Bentham, who argued that 'community is a fiction',[22] Thatcher infamously declared that there was no such thing as society.[23] New Labour seemed determined to prove her wrong and moved towards a more communitarian approach. Influenced by the work of 'responsive communitarians' writing in the last decade of the twentieth century, in particular the prolific writer Amitai Etzioni,[24] the then Government ushered in various criminal justice measures that had at their heart an emphasis on restoration and reparation, and a balancing of rights and responsibilities. There were various grassroots forces behind the rise of restorative justice, including faith-based and abolitionist influences, but communitarianism was the primary political philosophy guiding restorative measures.

Communitarians recognise that people are social animals with a need for affective attachments and responsibilities to one another. They bemoan the growing fragmentation of societies and argue for public measures to protect and enhance social responsibility and community life. This not only has implications for the planning and development of geographical locations, but also feeds into 'nation-building' exercises and policies to promote links to kinship and identity groups. Some measures, in the communitarian worldview, cannot be left to the state but must be organised *by* citizens *for* citizens. Responsive communitarians do not reject the values of human rights and liberty, but they argue that alone these are insufficient; that commitment to the common good is also necessary, and ways and means must be established to reconcile rights, liberty

---

[22] J Bentham, *An Introduction to the Principles of Morals and Legislation* (New York, Doubleday, Doran and Co, 1935) 8.

[23] M Thatcher, *The Downing Street Years* (London, Harper Collins, 1993) 626.

[24] Key texts from this period include: A Etzioni, *The Spirit of the Community* (New York, Crown Publishers, 1993) and *The New Golden Rule* (New York, Basic Books, 1996); D Bell, *Communitarianism and Its Critics* (Oxford, Clarendon Press, 1993); and, a little later, P Selznick, *The Communitarian Persuasion* (Washington, DC, Woodrow Wilson Center Press, 2002).

and the common good. Motivated by a sense of civic duty, communitarians seek ways of balancing individual rights with social responsibilities—the aim of various New Labour initiatives and the sentiments behind that government's discourses on criminal justice, particularly during Blair's administration.

This is not the place to present an overview of communitarianism, nor to discuss the tensions inherent in the communitarian ideals or their conflicts with liberal ideology.[25] Rather, it is simply to suggest that it is not accidental that restorative justice became popular at the same time as the rise of this second wave of communitarianism. Communitarians are keen to revitalise civil society, to introduce or strengthen opportunities for democratic participation of the public in social life; to increase mutual responsibilities and encourage collective cohesion. Restorative justice appeals to communitarians because it is about decentralisation, informality and participation, and because it provides a promising mechanism for promoting social responsibility. In the communitarian model, justice is not something done *to* the community or *for* the community but rather *with* the community. It is not about the state imposing solutions on individuals but rather about empowering participants to find solutions—the very aim of restorative justice.

Communitarians believe in the capacity for policies and institutions to enhance the moral infrastructure of communities and to transmit values from generation to generation. They are interested in the ways in which collective norms and values are shaped and transmitted through schools, families and other communities or networks by the strength of the 'moral voice'.[26] They celebrate the value of informal sanctioning that takes place in schools, families and neighbourhoods, where moral messages are passed on in contexts which give space to emotion. Not surprisingly, there is faith in the ability of communities to respond adequately to at least some transgressions through censure, judgement and appropriate punishment, without exclusion or denigration, and without the need to

---

[25] Adam Crawford has published various persuasive critiques of communitarianism in restorative justice (see the Bibliography to this work).

[26] Etzioni, *The Spirit of the Community*, above n 24, at 31.

involve the coercive state. The courts are seen as too formal, too hierarchical and too authoritarian, whereas restorative processes use communal and informal means of censuring behaviour and resocialising those who transgress the norms of society. Restorative justice holds the promise of drawing on communities to challenge transgressions and re-educate or re-socialise their members, with minimal state control or interference. Given some communitarians' mistrust of state power, there was obvious appeal in engaging civil society in a dialogic process; in bringing together victims, offenders and other members of their community, or communities, to consider appropriate responses to crime.

The flaw in the communitarian approach is its tendency to throw the proverbial baby out with the bathwater; the communitarian concern about corrosive state power has led some restorativists to reject outright the legitimacy of any role for the state in responding to crime. Indeed, communitarianism's hostility to state power might help to explain why, when it came to it, England's New Labour Government was happy to co-opt communitarianism and restorative rhetoric and restorative practice in the shallow end of criminal justice, but not to concede their reality—which determines a reduction in state power. For less cynical reasons, it is here that, having taken the best of the communitarian agenda, I also part company with them.

Rejection of state legitimacy is rooted in an 'othering' of the state, as unhelpful as the 'othering' of those who transgress. It seems that for many communitarians the state has nothing to do with 'us'; that citizens and communities are not intrinsically bound up in the state. This misconception conspires against a perceptive and appreciative account of criminal justice as well as restorative justice. Citizens have a relationship directly with the state and vice versa: both have responsibilities and rights in relation to the other. Citizens also have a relationship with various different communities and, again, commitments and responsibilities go in both directions. But there are limitations to the responsibilities of the community towards individual citizens, whereas the state has legally binding responsibilities towards all citizens. What is more, citizens have rights—

non-derogable rights—that are provided for by the state, and not by communities. It is for these reasons that citizens need relationships both with their communities and with the state. This need is not so apparent in our day-to-day lives, but becomes highly pertinent when something—in this example, crime—disrupts our personal status quo. It is for this reason that I argue that whilst low-level crimes and disorders can be resolved adequately within the community, by restorative means, more serious violations require that the state assumes a role; whether that be in investigating crime and prosecuting offenders, or in providing compensation for victims, or in punishing offenders, or only in keeping a check on the administration of justice within the community.

It might be helpful in explaining why the state has a justifiable role in communitarian forms of justice to provide a couple of examples of restorative processes with state oversight. One well-known example is provided by the response to youth crime in New Zealand. Whilst very serious offences are dealt with by way of restorative family group conferences, and whilst the community involved agree on the outcome of the meeting, meetings are managed by a state department (the Department of Child, Youth and Family Services) and are conducted within the legal framework of the Children, Young Persons and Their Families Act 1989. Hence the state has some control over the process, in that participants are required to pay due regard to the interests of the victim in agreeing an outcome plan, a plan which can be reviewed by a judge. In this example, whilst the community is the key decision maker, the state oversees and has some influence on its decisions. This scheme therefore gives space to communitarian aims, whilst providing the protections that come with state oversight of the process and outcomes.

The second example is provided by 'circles of support and accountability' (COSA), a restorative approach to the risk management of high-risk sexual offenders which emerged in Canada in the mid-1990s and was introduced into the Thames Valley area of England in 2002. The COSA provide support and advocacy for sex offenders released into the community following a term in prison.

In doing so, they aim to enhance the safety of the community and particularly vulnerable groups. As with other restorative measures, the COSA hold offenders (in this case ex-offenders) accountable for the harms they have done and for behaving responsibly in future. The relationship between the COSA and the state is different in Canada from that in the UK and US, but in all schemes there is a legitimate role for both community and state. In Canada screened and trained volunteers comprise an inner circle of community support for the ex-offender (the 'core member'). This scheme is outside of the criminal justice system and the volunteers deal directly with the core member, but they themselves draw on advice and support from an outer circle of professionals. Whilst the professional group is also drawn from the community, its members are at a distance from the core member and can be seen as a resource for the volunteers and the community more widely. They represent, in essence, a safety net. Other schemes (for example, in the Thames Valley) operate within the criminal justice system (under the aegis of the multi-agency public protection arrangements). The professionals, who more clearly represent the state, work directly with the core member to provide appropriate treatment with the aim of reducing the likelihood of reoffending, whilst the community circle of volunteers provides the core member with support and gradually try to reintegrate him into the community.

The professionals have a responsibility to the volunteers and the core members, but also to the wider society. Furthermore, the core member has certain rights, for example not to be abused and not to have his freedom limited beyond what has been imposed first by the state, in the post-release plan, and then by agreement between the core member and the inner circle of volunteers or, in some jurisdictions, the professional members. If relationships within the inner circle break down, the core member has the right to receive further support from the state, and the state has the obligation to provide this or to punish breaches of post-release licence conditions by the offender. Hence, this example shows how the lines of accountability, responsibility and rights within restorative processes do not end at the level of community.

Restorative justice—with its inclusionary emphasis on promoting mutual respect, empathetic exchanges and restoration of relationships—seems to be anomalous in the current 'risk society', with its emphasis on excluding and protecting ourselves against those who threaten our sense of security or are feared because they appear to be different. Nor does restorative justice's focus on responding to crime through community dialogue and consensus (a form of communitarian crime control) cohere well with the growing significance of individualistic legal protection under the human rights agenda. But the above examples suggest that communitarian values can drive our response to crime and disorder, while libertarian protections curb the excesses of communitarian fervour. Whilst human rights can provide a safety net beneath which protection for individual liberty should not fall, there remains scope for processes influenced by communitarianism and orientated towards the promotion of social justice—in other words, opportunities for communities to respond to crime and disorder by mobilising shared norms and other forms of informal social control. Restorative justice is an attractive prospect for those who do not subscribe to the 'criminology of the other' and who yearn for a more humanised response to crime.

V. RESTORATIVE JUSTICE AND CRIMINAL JUSTICE: COMPLEMENTARY NOT CONTRADICTORY

A. A Challenge to an Unhelpful Dichotomy

Early proselytising restorativists were determined to contrast restorative justice with retributive justice, which, because of its focus on acts against the state, was seen as denying justice to victims and their communities. Restorative justice, on the other hand, was praised for positing crime as 'a violation of people and relationships' which 'creates obligations to make things right'.[27] In

---

[27] H Zehr, *Changing Lenses: A New Focus for Crime and Justice* (Scottdale, Pa, Herald Press, 1990; revised 1995) 181.

1990, having pointed out everything that was wrong with retribution and right with restoration, Howard Zehr inaugurated what has since become something of a restorative justice fanfare by suggesting that it could become a fully-functioning alternative to established criminal justice, a 'new lens' through which to perceive crime. Others with an abolitionist bent further developed Zehr's dichotomy, insisting societies choose between the two 'alternatives'. Some even dragged gender into their arsenal of weapons against conventional justice systems, suggesting that responses to crime could be divided along gender lines: with criminal justice following the Portia (masculine) model, which emphasises abstract, rational and rights-based thinking, and restorative justice following the Persephone (feminine) model, which is inspired by an 'ethics of care' and is contextual and relational.[28]

The retributive/restorative justice dichotomy fast became the standard (oppositional) approach used to define restorative justice. The two systems were regarded as fundamentally opposed, not only because one is relational and the other is not but because, by and large, advocates of restorative justice believed that it had nothing to do with sentencing and punishment, and that criminal justice had no restorative elements. It was argued that even when the sanctions each imposed were superficially similar, they stemmed from different forms of intent. Retributive justice was dismissed as merely punitive; a contemporary version of the biblical view of proportionality ('an eye for an eye, a tooth for a tooth'). In contrast, restorative justice was not thought to be punitive because it was not *intended* to inflict pain but to be constructive and healing.

Debates between 'rival champions' of restoration and retribution prompted some in the academy to contemplate this emergence of apparently polarised positions and argue that reparation is in fact reconcilable with retribution.[29] And while some proponents

---

[28] G Masters and D Smith 'Portia and Persephone revisited: thinking about feeling in criminal justice' (1998)2(1) *Theoretical Criminology*, 5.

[29] L Zedner 'Reparation and Retribution: Are They Reconcilable?' (1994) 57(2) *MLR*, 228.

of the antithetical view of restorative and retributive justice remain entrenched in their respective positions, more recently there have been further efforts to bridge the gap, and in some cases to see restoration and retribution as integrally linked. Indeed the legal philosopher, Antony Duff, has argued persuasively for 'restoration through retribution': 'offenders should suffer retribution, punishment, for their crimes, but the essential purpose of such punishment should be to achieve restoration.'[30]

Restoration and retribution are not contradictory. Both are essential in the pursuit of justice for offenders, victims and communities harmed by crime and disorder. Retributive punishment not only takes place in the criminal justice system, it also occurs in restorative processes. Where offenders have damaged their relationships with the victim and others in their community, the appropriate (desert-based) response is to confront those offenders with their wrongdoing and encourage them to recognise and repent the culpable wrong they have committed. This will inevitably involve a process of retributive censure, which can be achieved by citizens coming together to discuss the harms done in a restorative conference. This process can be, and often is, experienced by the offender, and even his or her supporters, as painful.

Repentance must be demonstrated by the offender seeking to restore the bonds of community damaged by the offending behaviour. An apology (to the victim and to others) is the minimum reparative requirement, but this can be supplemented by an agreement to make material compensation or carry out work for the victim or wider community in order that reparation is commensurate with the seriousness of the offence. What is more, this process of secular penance usually involves a commitment by the offender not to repeat the offence, and sometimes even to seek or accept help that might be needed in order to prevent reoffending. Thus restorative processes can result in forms of rehabilitation. Having completed the restorative intervention, other citizens typically feel

[30] R A Duff, 'Restorative Punishment and Punitive Restoration' in L Walgrave (ed), *Restorative Justice and the Law* (Cullompton, Willan Publishing, 2002) 82.

obliged to offer to the offender reconciliation and restoration of the bonds of community.

The intentional and authoritative imposition of a burden on an offender in response to a breach of the criminal law qualifies a process as punitive. Restorative processes can impose considerable burdens on offenders and so unequivocally deliver punishment. Whether that burden is motivated by a desire to cause the offender to suffer or experience pain is not determinative, neither is it a necessary quality of punishment that it actually be experienced as painful. Furthermore, retributivists typically include forms of moral communication, indeed moral condemnation—such as censure—in their theories. Given that the process and outcome of restorative justice can be characterised as a form of moral communication involving the imposition of burdens on offenders, it must be that both retribution and restoration can, and usually do, occur in restorative practices.

At the same time, restorative measures may be found in court-based retributive processes. Courts do not sentence defendants in the absence of relevant information about the context within which the offence was committed and the relevant personal history of the defendant. Typically, court-appointed probation officers, prosecutors and defence solicitors will present mitigating or aggravating factors to the court that are not entirely dissimilar to the information provided to a conference by supporters of both victims and offenders and by the wider community. Such information helps judges, juries and magistrates, just as it does participants in conferences, better to understand the culpability of the offender and the seriousness of the offence, and, consequently, to adjudge the proportionate penalty. More obviously, victim impact statements read out to the court, either by the victim or by his or her representative, are a more formal mechanism for the victim's rights to allocution within the conference.

Some have argued that the main distinction between court and conference is found in the level of emotion present and, more importantly, expected or tolerated. However, as the work of Susanne Karstedt and others has shown, there is a good deal of emotion in the courtroom and, by and large, the criminal justice system can, and does, cope with it.[31] And, finally, courts have clear mechanisms for compensating victims. Whilst compensation is court-imposed, rather than negotiated by the relevant community, it does, nonetheless, go some way to repairing the harms caused by crimes.

While there is by no means consensus on the compatibility of restorative and retributive justice, it is clear that restorative justice (on the whole) does not reject all punitive measures associated with retributive justice and that the court system is not devoid of all restorative elements. There is more common ground between the two forms of justice than is often recognised. As others have argued, restorative justice is not an alternative *to* punishment but an alternative form *of* punishment.[32]

B. The Case for the Coexistence of Restorative and Criminal Justice

Given that retributive justice can comprise some restorative measures, and that restorative justice can and does punish offenders, it is not inevitable that certain crimes should be dealt with restoratively and others by way of prosecution and the courts. Restorative justice generally pre-supposes that the offender has acknowledged responsibility for an offence. In other words, it is not concerned with fact-finding but with an appropriate response to an admitted offence. Its realm is that of sentencing, not that of the criminal trial. Hence, where an offender does not plead guilty to a criminal charge, he or she is destined for the courts. Of course, this does not preclude a restorative response: once there is a finding of guilt, a restorative intervention can replace other disposals, such as prison,

---

[31] S Karstedt, 'Emotions and criminal justice' (2002) 6(3) *Theoretical Criminology*, 299.

[32] See the work of Kathy Daly and of Lode Walgrave, referred to in the Bibliography to this work. This section draws on work with Richard Young, previously published in R Young and C Hoyle, 'Restorative Justice and Punishment' in S McConville (ed), *The Use of Punishment* (Cullompton, Willan, 2003).

fines or community sentences, or it can be in addition to other disposals. So where and how should restorative justice operate?

The most common fears amongst liberals centre on the danger that restorative justice will result in 'net-widening': dragging into the justice system people or behaviours that would otherwise be left alone on the grounds that the system has something beneficial to offer them. It is easy to argue that restorative justice processes bring benefits to those involved, including the offenders. It is, for most of us, rather difficult to make such claims for prison. Hence, restorative justice might pose a threat to the liberal goal of penal moderation. The challenge therefore is to include restorative justice in the penal arsenal for serious as well as minor offences, without adding further to penal excess.[33]

Restorative justice has been shown to have enormous potential in dealing with conflicts in schools and neighbourhoods, particularly for anti-social behaviours that do not warrant a criminal justice response. Most parts of the UK have experimented with restorative conferencing for disputes where no criminal offence has yet taken place, or where it is not considered expedient to caution or prosecute anyone. 'Community conferences' run along similar lines to restorative conferences for victims and offenders, albeit with a greater emphasis on including community residents and representatives, and provide an effective and reintegrative response to community problems. Such problems include neighbourhood disputes, 'quality of life offences'—such as public drinking or being 'drunk and disorderly', graffiti, vandalism or begging[34]—and even (non-criminal) racist incidents. Community conferences can be particularly appropriate for 'signal crimes'. These are criminal and disorderly incidents that shape local communities' perceptions of risks to their security in everyday life. A sense that the very fabric of their community is being changed

---

[33] For a persuasive account of penal excess, see Loader, above n 7.

[34] Whilst most such offences are dealt with by way of an informal warning or police caution in the UK, they often result in prosecution in certain US states such as New York, where a 'zero-tolerance' approach has led to extremely disproportionate responses to young people putting their feet on subway seats, for example.

(for the worse) by such acts and behaviour, and that repeated incidents are highly likely, reduces communities' feelings of safety and security, causing them to change the way they behave. If people hear about or witness such incidents in their local community, they may feel less safe and therefore move away, or avoid particular locations or people. Alternatively, they could decide to respond by exclusionary or vigilante behaviour.[35] Community conferencing has the potential to reduce fear, disruption and reciprocal aggression for signal crimes.

For some time now, restorative conferencing has been used to tackle various types of harmful behaviour within schools, including bullying, assaults and damage to school property, usually with assistance from community police officers. Some schools aim to integrate restorative principles into most of their day-to-day activities, whilst others use family group conferencing only to deal with specific, and sometimes more serious, incidents. The techniques used to conference youths who have been accused of bullying, being very disruptive or damaging property within the school are remarkably similar to restorative conferences between victims and offenders within the criminal process. Research has shown that such processes promote harmonious relationships in school, and typically bring about the successful resolution of conflict and harm. These community-based initiatives provide an opportunity to break with the increasingly litigious and exclusionary approaches that are the typical recourse of citizens and agencies alike. Too often young people who get into trouble at school are excluded, usually temporarily at first but then, with little positive intervention, often permanently. Excluded children are more likely to come into contact with the criminal justice system, and some will end up serving short prison sentences that cause disproportionate disruption to their lives and damage their prospects. Rather than restorative responses in these areas leading to net-widening, they might well divert some cases from the criminal justice system. But by and large,

---

[35] See the work of Martin Innes, for example M Innes 'Signal crimes and signal disorders: notes on deviance as communicative action' (2004) 55(3) *The British Journal of Sociology*, 335.

for all but the most serious offences restorative justice will operate within the criminal process, and indeed it should, as the justice system is able to provide the due process safeguards not available within a purely communitarian model of restorative justice.

Restorative justice can play a role in responses to most offences, from shop theft, through violence in the home, to crimes against humanity. Each of these, and other offences, will likely require different combinations, or a different balance, of restorative and retributive justice. For most property offences—with the exception of serious or organised property crime—restorative justice will often be all that is necessary. For violent offences, retribution might require a prison sentence combined with one or more restorative encounters.

Retribution and restoration might be reconcilable in theory, but how should complementary justice be delivered in practice? For example, how would the outcome of one type of justice (whether that be a restorative conference or a prison sentence) impact on decisions about the other? Should a prison sentence tariff be reduced if an offender cooperates with a restorative process and complies fully and enthusiastically with a reparation agreement? Should only those who behave well in prison and successfully complete rehabilitation programs have the opportunity to engage in restorative processes? And, of course, how should we decide when sentences are required in addition to a restorative encounter? It is essential to adopt a principled normative position on such matters, as social scientific research on efficacy might well lead us astray. If we turn to the current empirical evidence provided by randomised controlled experiments comparing restorative and retributive justice, we find that for violent crimes and crimes where there is a personal victim, restorative justice is most effective (in terms of victim satisfaction and reducing reoffending) when used in *addition* to retributive justice; for example, restorative conferencing as part of a prison sentence, or as well as a fine.[36] This might well be

---

[36] L Sherman and H Strang, *Restorative Justice: The Evidence* (London, The Smith Institute, 2007).

optimal for victims and even for reducing offending, but it does not sit comfortably with the goal of penal moderation. The imposition of financial penalties on offenders whose prospects of desistance are not dramatically improved by such punishment, or the further over-burdening of our prisons with offenders who could safely serve their sentence in the community, provide no benefits and can result in some considerable costs to both the individuals involved and society more generally. The decision to incarcerate someone, even someone who has committed a serious offence, should be a difficult one. Prison is painful, not just for the offender but for the family and community he or she leaves behind. It can, and often does, do damage to many, and so restraint in sentencing is essential. The choice to imprison needs to be justified by reference both to the unavailability or exhaustion of alternatives and the culpability of the offender and the harms caused by his or her actions.

Some restorativists have adopted a 'pyramid approach' to sentencing in order to explore how restorative, deterrent and incapacitative justice may be integrated. Under most of such 'responsive regulation'[37] approaches the offender is given the chance of restorative justice for a first offence. If he fails to comply or to desist from offending, the state response becomes more onerous, until finally the incompetent or irrational offender is incapacitated for failing to respond appropriately to lesser punishments. In this model, prison is the ultimate threat hanging over those who are offered restorative approaches.

I prefer a system that does not offer restorative justice only as a first chance but rather chooses the more appropriate justice response to each offence, even if that means offering repeated

---

[37] John Braithwaite has written extensively on responsive regulation in restorative justice processes. He explains that 'The basic idea of responsive regulation is that governments should be responsive to the conduct of those they seek to regulate in deciding whether a more or less interventionist response is needed. In particular law enforcers should be responsive to how effectively citizens or corporations are regulating themselves before deciding whether to escalate intervention.' J Braithwaite, *Restorative Justice and Responsive Regulation* (Oxford, Oxford University Press, 2002) at 29.

restorative meetings if each individual offence deserves no mo... Even committed restorativists have in the main avoided recommending this. For them, restorative justice is seen as a 'chance', a reward for first-time or juvenile offenders. If the offender goes on to reoffend they concede defeat, and shrug as the courts respond by ratcheting up the penalties. The message is that restorative justice failed to rehabilitate or deter so we should try something else. This, of course, is not the response to the high levels of recidivism after incarceration. The courts do not refuse to send people back to prison because prison failed to deter the first time around: indeed, not only do they continue to incarcerate ex-prisoners, but in most cases they also increase the length of sentence and often put the offender in a higher category prison to further restrict his freedoms or privileges. I propose that restorative justice should not be a 'one chance and you're out' option but that it should be available when it is the appropriate response to an offence, even if the offender has failed to desist after repeated restorative meetings. This is because it is naive to believe that a one-off restorative conference can bring about immediate and permanent desistance in the absence of significant cultural and structural changes to reduce the criminogenic nature of offenders' lives. It might for some, but not for most. However, repeated restorative encounters just might help to support those who are inclined towards desistance. As it is almost impossible to identify those, as most offenders will *claim* to be in this camp, the opportunity must be given to all. Furthermore, in many cases repeated offences will be against different victims. If restorative justice is beneficial to victims—and the evidence points in this direction—why deny the process to a victim of a second-, third- or ninth-time offender? To do so is to prove what many already suspect; that measures introduced by governments under the victims' banner often have a rather different rationale.

I suggest that restorative justice is used for repeat and for 'deep end' offences and offenders, including serious and even, in some cases, sexually violent offences. I acknowledge, therefore, that in a great many of the more serious cases (although not necessarily the repeat cases) the offender will need to be imprisoned to protect the public or for the purpose of retribution. However, this combined approach can be justified only if we think parsimoniously about the retributive sentence, if, in other words, we reduce the tariff accordingly. This of course raises objections of disproportionality in sentencing, if those offenders whose victims are willing and able to meet with them get lighter tariffs. This then raises questions about whether victims should have a choice about whether or not to participate in restorative processes. Each answer gives rise to further questions and makes clear the need to give serious and careful consideration to how a complementary approach to justice should operate: to think through what the dangers are, and therefore what the safeguards should be, and consider how to prevent the compromise of a liberal commitment to penal moderation.

C. A Framework for the Coexistence of Restorative and Criminal Justice

This section will explore how a complementary approach to justice might look, considering some of the key questions that have led others to conclude that retribution and restoration are incompatible:

a) Who should be invited to participate in a restorative intervention?
b) Should participation be compulsory for some?
c) How can restorative sentences be made commensurate with the seriousness of the offence?
d) Who should facilitate restorative processes?

1. *Engaging community: in search of appropriate participants*

Since the publication of John Braithwaite's seminal text, *Crime, Shame and Reintegration,*[38] restorativists have debated the meaning of the concept 'reintegration'. The ostensible aim of restorative processes—to reintegrate offenders back into their communi-

---

[38] J Braithwaite, *Crime, Shame and Reintegration* (Cambridge, Cambridge University Press, 1989).

ties—assumes two things. First, it assumes that there is a community of law-abiding—or at least pro-social—people into which offenders can be reintegrated. And, secondly, it assumes that if only these people will open their arms and forgive the aberrations of the offender, he or she will be able to resume his or her place in that nurturing community. These assumptions raise issues of practical concern: What is the appropriate community? Who should the facilitator invite to participate in the meeting and support the offender? And how can their engagement with the offender be facilitated? But the assumptions also raise issues of philosophical concern: is it the role of criminal or community justice to go beyond punishing people for infractions of the criminal law and make judgements about which features of offenders' lives might be criminogenic in order to restructure their relationships within their communities and alter their, and even others', behaviours?

Strict retributivists will likely disapprove of attempts to 'engineer' social, community or familial relationships with the aim of reintegrating offenders into law-abiding communities. However, those who are sympathetic to rehabilitative goals will recognise that such attempts by restorative facilitators, or other participants, are not dissimilar to the aims of probation officers (including—to a lesser extent—those in custodial settings) in their one-to-one relationships with clients. They too attempt to nurture or even create the conditions for successful integration into pro-social communities through a mixture of formal requirements (breaches of which can attract further punishment) and informal measures to encourage the development or maintenance of 'appropriate' relationships. Rehabilitative measures in prisons—anger-management, cognitive behavioural or life-skills programmes for offenders—similarly have at their heart the aim to reintegrate offenders into law-abiding communities upon their release. These attempts too often fail to realise their potential because they do not typically engage those parties— beyond the prison—best able to facilitate and support change. Restorative justice is not a menacing form of social engineering, or even community meddling, aimed at denying the legitimacy of cultures alien to the mainstream. Rather, it is a means of identifying the negative influences on those who commit offences and of providing options for participating in community life that avoid causing harm to others. A young offender who socialises with a group of people regularly involved in crime can be introduced to alternative, lawful means of recreation, and to opportunities for establishing or building on relationships with pro-social people. Alternatively, he or she may be advised of means of resisting peer pressure to deviate, or even of providing a positive influence on others in his or her immediate community who continue to transgress. Restorative responses can be tailored to suit the unique characteristics of offenders and their social and familial circumstances to put them on the right path, as long as they appropriately engage with the community.

Turning to more practical concerns, research has shown us that the dynamics of a successful restorative intervention are dependent on the facilitator having identified the most suitable participants, invited them to the meeting, and encouraged challenging and yet respectful interaction between all parties. Identifying the right supporters for victims is reasonably straightforward where there is not a pre-existing close relationship between the victim and offender. Most often these are the partners, spouses, siblings, parents or friends of victims. As part of their kinship community, these people are likely to be best able to support the victim throughout the meeting and for some time following. Complications can arise where the victim and offender share the same community—are members of the same family, school, workplace or close friendship group. In such cases the appropriate supporters for the victim could well be the best choice for the offender, raising the problem of mixed loyalties or conflicts of interest. A skilled facilitator will invite those most keen to assist, comfort or encourage either of the main actors, but with the aim of mobilising support for both from these participants and developing dialogue about the harms done to the whole community, including the supporters themselves. Such conferences can be extremely successful because of the enhanced prospect of offenders being held accountable by all participants, and by the genuine willingness of the community to reintegrate a contrite offender. Nonetheless, they do require careful planning and management so as to avoid either the offender or the victim feeling isolated within the meeting.

Connection to a community facilitates the development of supportive and reciprocal social networks that benefit both the group and its members, something that is known as 'social capital'. Some restorative sceptics suggest that certain neglected communities, characterised by extreme socio-economic deprivation, have been so blighted by crime, anti-social behaviour and resulting anomie, that there exists no social capital, no meaningful community on which to draw. Such concerns probably reflect a middle-class, even ethnocentric notion of community. In such areas the driveways of houses or the stairways of tower blocks may well be cluttered with land-fill debris and stained with offensive graffiti; there is highly unlikely to be a functioning neighbourhood watch scheme, and dangerous dogs—rather than shiny new cars–might be the street status symbol. But this does not mean that the social fabric of life has collapsed entirely, that there is no trust or social capital and that the inhabitants care nothing for each other.[39] It might provide something of a challenge for facilitators to identify those people from that community who do not share the offender's norms and values, and who do not excuse or even approve of the harmful behaviour. Nonetheless, in most cases facilitators will manage to locate appropriate pro-social supporters for offenders, whether they are grandparents, teachers, social workers, reformed drug addicts or local football coaches.

Of course, whilst such people can provide avenues for rehabilitation, they may not so easily be able to provide reintegration into the most crucial communities for offenders—most typically kinship or friendship groups—if those closest to the offender share his or her standpoint. Hence, it may sometimes also be necessary to invite these people to the restorative meeting, despite

---

[39] Adrian Nicole LeBlanc's ethnographic tour de force, *Random Family*, shows that social capital can be found in the most deprived, crime-ridden community in the Bronx: *Random Family: Love, Drugs, Trouble, and Coming of Age in the Bronx* (New York, Scribner, 2004).

their apparently harmful influence. In such circumstances it may be appropriate for facilitators indirectly to challenge some of the norms and values of the wider community in encouraging offenders to reflect on and account for their behaviour, hence improving the prospects for the whole group, including the offender. As long as facilitators do not use a restorative process to investigate offences committed by those who are not within the purview of the criminal justice system, an intervention that goes beyond the prospects for the offender and discusses and advises on matters of wider social concern should not be considered to be beyond the pale.

Concerns about successful participation reflect not only middle-class biases about those lower down the social ladder, but also post-modern fears that across the classes, and perhaps especially amongst those in higher socio-economic brackets, there no longer exist communities to mobilise. This oft-stated objection to restorative justice reflects either a perception of an absence of communities, or a view of communities as exclusive, and even oppressive or intolerant of difference. The fear amongst sociologists is that social capital in modern societies is generally in decline. Hence some critics of restorative justice argue that whilst it might work for local indigenous communities, who exhibit tight social bonds, it has no currency in diverse and transitory post-modern societies.

However, although many people today do not regularly attend a place of worship or participate in group activities around sport or recreation that traditionally have taken place in 'community centres' or on local communal grounds, they are part of communities. They are more likely to be integrated into a network at their place of work or around their educational establishment, or in a friendship group tied by a shared mutual interest (witness the fairly recent trend for the establishment of book clubs) or shared responsibilities (for example parents of children in a local school). If these groups are integrated and have shared emotional as well as practical connections, they constitute a community, even if some prefer the word 'network'. Furthermore, even those who believe that modern Western societies have moved too far along the collec-tivist–individualist continuum[40] to render community meaningful, recognise that community brings values towards which we aspire.[41]

Defining places or people as 'within' the boundaries of a commu-nity necessarily excludes those outside. This is not a problem if people are excluded because they belong to a different 'legitimate' community: Jewish people will not feel insulted because they are not invited to pray in a Hindu temple; and residents of an old people's home will not feel harmed by not receiving an invitation to the annual meet of their local cricket club. But young, Asian men living in deprived inner-city areas might well feel aggrieved at being denied a short-cut to their destination because of the erection of an exclu-sive gated community. If one such man climbs over the gate and damages the residents' property, what kind of community would a restorative response aim to repair? The victims at such a meeting would not realistically be seeking to reintegrate the offender into *their* community. The communities of victims and offenders in such an example would rarely overlap. One group is held at a distance—either metaphorically or physically—by barriers.

Restorative justice cannot be conceived of as a mechanism for breaking down these barriers. Instead it must aim to do two things. First, and most obviously, it must repair damage done *within* these two communities. By including some of those from the communi-ties of both victim and offender, both can be supported. Whilst

---

[40] Collectivist societies, such as China, give primacy to the aspirations and welfare of groups and the relationships between people who are integrated into these cohe-sive groups. This is contrasted with the cultural trait of individualism, more typical of Western societies, with the USA usually cited as the most extreme example. Individualistic cultures are more self-centred: everyone is expected to look after him-self or herself and his or her immediate family only, with the ties between other indi-viduals being loose. In practice, most societies are not purely collectivist or individualist, but could be placed somewhere along the continuum between these two ways of functioning.

[41] Zygmunt Bauman, for example, notes that today we look for individual salvation from shared troubles, which leaves us feeling more, not less, insecure. Community, he argues, is a 'kind of world which is not, regrettably, available to us—but which we would dearly love to inhabit and which we hope to repossess': Z. Bauman, *Seeking Safety in an Insecure World* (Cambridge, Polity Press, 2001) 3.

there will be some in the communities from which the offender comes who feel his or her behaviour to be justified by societal neglect (poor education, poor social security, inadequate housing or transport, for example) or an iniquitous distribution of resources, others will condemn the criminal behaviour and be determined to hold the offender to account. These people can help to reintegrate the offender into a law-abiding and pro-social community.

Secondly, restorative justice must facilitate at least some understanding across the two communities. Whilst the offender and victim might be worlds apart in terms of access to economic, cultural and perhaps even emotional resources, restorative processes can appeal to common humanity, to common values of honesty, caring and personal integrity. It can facilitate a dialogue that reduces social distance, even if not permanently. In modern Western societies where certain youths are regarded with suspicion and fear, and even seen by some as 'feral', this is imperative.

Whilst concerns have been expressed, and presumptions made, about supporters on 'sink estates', little ink has been spilled on the subject of the suitability of parents, whether middle class or working class, as supporters of young offenders, and yet these relationships can adversely affect the dynamics of the process. Contrary to majority assumptions, some parents of young offenders are not best placed to act as their sole supporters through a restorative conference. This is because the process may be too painful for them, as they are the very people who feel most responsible for the offenders. Messages aimed at highlighting the offender's moral responsibility find currency with parents in a way that makes them feel ashamed, embarrassed and as if they themselves are on trial. Parents react to this discomfort by engaging in apologising, neutralising, dominating and punitive discourses. Their reactions not only cast doubt upon their ability to be composed and supportive of their children, but, more importantly, might also adversely affect the conference dynamics.

Parental reactions might thereby deny the young person the opportunity to take responsibility for his or her actions and to contribute to the discussion on appropriate reparation, which could ultimately thwart his or her chance for reintegration. Parents often feel guilty and responsible for their children's actions because they see them as a product of their own genes, lifestyles, parenting skills and values, and therefore often apologise or make excuses for their children's actions, leaving young offenders free to absolve themselves of responsibility. Such tactics can, without appropriate checks and balances, lead to disproportionately low reparation agreements, or even to parents carrying out reparation on behalf of their children. Parents of a young offender should usually be asked to attend a restorative meeting, but not necessarily as the sole supporters of the offender, rather as part of the close community harmed by an offence. In this sense they should be seen, in many cases, as secondary victims, who may well need their own supporters with them. Clearly there needs to be a move away from the automatic assumption that full parental involvement in restorative processes is always in the best interests of offenders, or, for that matter, parents.[42]

Whilst we have ideas about who can or should be invited to participate in restorative meetings in order to realise the potential of the process, we also know, from empirical studies, that often people are reluctant to attend. How should such reluctance be managed?

2. *A qualified defence of coercion*

One of the key principles of restorative justice, espoused by early advocates, is voluntariness. Indeed, restorative orthodoxy holds that nobody should be coerced into participating in a restorative meeting—particularly the victim, but also the offender. This is justified in terms of avoiding re-victimisation: it is thought that those offenders who are unwilling to participate would be less likely to take responsibility for their actions and make reparative gestures, and perhaps be more likely to be truculent. Conversely, voluntariness has never been a cornerstone of criminal justice: courts can

---

[42] C Hoyle and S Noguera 'Supporting Young Offenders Through Restorative Justice: Parents as (In)Appropriate Adults' (2008)6(3) *British Journal of Community Justice* 67.

compel victims and other witnesses to testify, and sometimes, often controversially, punish those victims who refuse to cooperate with the criminal process. And although offenders do not have to assist their own defence, they cannot opt out of the criminal process if they are charged with a crime. Few have considered whether this discrepancy is defensible.

When restorative justice is available as a diversion from prosecution, the issue of defendant compellability is not so pertinent. If an offender chooses not to participate, he or she will likely be prosecuted in court, or will receive a warning or police caution without a restorative element, if this is proportionate to the offence. But if restorative justice is part of the sentence of a court, refusal to participate in a restorative meeting is rather tricky. Offenders cannot opt out of prison or of a community service order, so there would seem to be no clear justification for allowing them to opt out of a restorative meeting. Of course, one practical solution to reluctant offenders would be to link the restorative encounter to the 'retributive sentence'. Within such a scheme, restorative and retributive elements would be presented as a sentence deal: if the defendant cooperates with the restorative process, he or she will receive a lesser retributive sentence; a non-custodial rather than custodial sentence, a shorter prison term, or a less demanding or intrusive community penalty. This would keep the sentence proportionate to the harms done (see section V.C.3. below) and provide an incentive for offenders to meet with their victims.

In the absence of such 'inducements', and in the face of a resistant offender, choices must be made by facilitators, for if we allow offenders' preferences to take precedence we necessarily deny victims the opportunities to participate in a process that might bring them some relief. Hence, whilst in an ideal world coercion would be used sparingly, if restorative and criminal justice are to coexist it will be necessary to coerce offenders in some cases, where they are not perceived to be determined to revictimise. However, where it is genuinely believed that an unwilling offender would use the restorative encounter to intimidate or in another way further harm the victim, coercion should be avoided and the retributive 'sentence discount' lost.

It is not necessary, though, to coerce victims, and there is no justification in doing so 'for their own good' or for the good of the state. Victims can be coerced to testify in court as their participation might be essential for the successful prosecution of the offender. Conversely, restorative justice generally pre-supposes that the offender has already acknowledged responsibility for an offence. It is not concerned with fact-finding but with an appropriate response to an admitted offence. So while victims are necessary to provide evidence to help juries and magistrates to decide on guilt or innocence in a criminal trial, they have no such role in a restorative encounter. While some facilitators might think that a restorative meeting would help a victim to achieve 'closure', they should not coerce a disinclined victim to participate with this aim in mind; neither should they do so to help to rehabilitate the offender. Victims should be given all the information they need to make an informed choice about participation but, once made, their choices should be respected.

However, reluctance to attend a restorative meeting should not deny victims the potential benefits of a restorative process. At its best, restorative justice can alleviate victims' feelings of anger or fear towards the offender and result in reparation. If possible, they should be able to enjoy these benefits by a process of shuttle mediation, even if they choose not to meet with the offender. Shuttle or indirect mediation requires the facilitator to feed the views of the victim into the meeting and then, after the meeting, relay back to the victim what the offender and other participants discussed, their responses to the victim (impact) statement and their proposals for making good the harms done. In some cases there is further mediated dialogue between the main parties. Research suggests that the less satisfactory outcomes of shuttle mediation may well be an inevitable result of the non-dynamic nature of limited participation: some people remain unconvinced by second-hand information and unmoved by messages conveyed by another person. However, it has also made clear that with effective facilitation, some of the benefits of restorative justice can be realised without a meeting between the victim and offender.[43]

3. *The aims of punishment and the boundaries of proportionality*

Critics of restorative justice tend to fall into one of two camps: some reject its fundamental principles because they compete with their own; others reject it because in practice it can sometimes go wrong. Some within the former camp use these examples of failure to support their (principled) case.

The first type of critic typically adheres to a 'just deserts' philosophy of retributivism that cannot accommodate restorative justice. Their belief that sentences should be commensurate with the seriousness of the offence is challenged by the participation of victims and members of the wider community in sentencing decisions. They are particularly concerned about the threat of disproportionate reparation agreements, but they also worry that within schemes where only those offenders whose victims agree to participate in a meeting have access to restorative justice, some offenders may receive harsher sentences than others. Where victims are given a choice it is inevitable that similarly culpable offenders, who are equally willing and able to participate in a restorative encounter, will be sentenced inequitably because of the victim's decision about participation. There are three possible responses to this. First, one can shrug and remark that such are the inequities of life. This of course does not get us very far. Secondly, a 'retributive sentence' discount could be given for willingness to participate in a conference, even if it later becomes clear that it cannot proceed (offenders would need to be asked about participation before the victim so as not to lead them cynically to manipulate the process). Whilst such offenders might not receive a fully reduced tariff—as would those who participated in a conference—they would get some credit. A third option would be for restorative meetings to

---

[43] C Hoyle, 'Securing Restorative Justice for the Non-Participating Victims' in C Hoyle and R Young (eds), *New Visions of Crime Victims* (Oxford, Hart Publishing, 2002) 97.

proceed without the victim but with other members of the wider community harmed by the offence, as well as members of the offender's community. And, as discussed above, the victim might be persuaded to engage in 'shuttle mediation' without the requirement to meet the offender. In such cases the full discount should apply.

Concerns about disproportionate reparation agreements have agitated strict retributivists to a greater degree but do not resonate with many restorativists, who consider that restorative justice and proportionality are fundamentally incompatible and are happy to dismiss the latter for the benefits of the former. They can accommodate reparation outcomes that are disproportionately harsh or soft, even if the extreme cases embarrass their cause. The now infamous Australian restorative cautioning case which resulted in a 12-year-old boy 'consenting' to parading outside the victim's shop wearing a t-shirt emblazoned with the words 'I am a Thief', became notorious because it was so crude and denigratory; but empirical research has shown other, more subtle examples of disproportionate and even inappropriate reparation agreements to which participants have apparently agreed. Two large retail stores in one American scheme frequently asked for 40 hours of community service to be written into reparation agreements, with one 13-year-old receiving this for the theft of a chocolate bar. Notwithstanding the concerns raised by such examples, the literature is replete with examples of 'appropriate' reparation agreements to (sometimes quite literally) repair the damage done—many involving requirements to paint a village hall defaced by graffiti, or to repair park furniture damaged by vandalism. Other examples of apparently proportionate agreements might involve a few hours of gardening, or the payment of insurance excess following the theft of a pedal cycle. And, by and large, empirical studies have found that most cases end with such agreements, rather than with overly punitive requirements imposed on offenders by vengeful victims.

The image of the vengeful victim and, to a lesser extent, exclusionary and punitive communities, drives concerns about disproportionate reparation agreements. But how realistic is this portrayal of victims and communities? It is true that in recent years many harsh, exclusionary measures introduced into the criminal justice systems in common law jurisdictions have been justified by reference to 'public opinion' and the demands of victims, but this is largely about political expediency, rather than a genuine response to the demands of those harmed by offending behaviour. If the public generally, and victims specifically, really were in favour of harsh punishments across the board, the arguments against providing victims and their supporters with any decisive say in sentencing become overwhelming, for that way lies the lynch mob. In fact, however, the evidence from many jurisdictions is that the public is much less vindictive than is commonly supposed, and that the more people know about the circumstances of an offence and an offender, the less punitive they tend to become. In other words, informed public opinion is very different from the 'gut reactions' tapped by general opinion polls or the media. When asked to specify a sentence for a hypothetical offender in a given set of circumstances, the public 'sentences' are broadly in line with actual court practices, and those who have recently been victims of the type of offence used in such exercises generally prove to be no more punitive than non-victims in this regard. When members of the public take on a decision-making role within criminal justice, as jurors or magistrates, their behaviour again contradicts the image of a universally punitive public.

So, to what philosophy of punishment does the public subscribe? When the views of members of the public are unpicked carefully, the great majority seem to favour proportionate sentencing based on the principle of just deserts. But they are also eclectic sentencers, in that they are interested in sentencing to prevent crime, and are also sensitive to victims' needs; if a particular sentence benefits the victim, members of the public are willing to forego imposing a proportional sentence.[44] We might therefore

---

[44] J V Roberts, M Hough, J Jacobson and N Moon, 'Public Attitudes to Sentencing Purposes and Sentencing Factors: An Empirical Analysis' [2009] *Crim LR* 771; J V Roberts and M Hough, *Understanding Public Attitudes to Criminal Justice* (Maidenhead, Open University Press, 2005) ch 7.

expect to find that when offenders and victims and their respective supporters come together in a setting which encourages respectful dialogue, the social distance between the participants narrows and demands for punishment become even more moderate, perhaps even to the point where lower proportionality limits are breached. Consistent with these expectations, empirical research has shown that restorative processes generally act, through mechanisms of deliberative accountability, to preclude disproportionately harsh outcomes. Further, that external review mechanisms (such as judicial oversight of conference outcomes) are typically used—if at all—to prevent outcomes that are too lenient. Nonetheless, such oversight is needed to cater for the occasional vengeful victim or community, or the conference agreement that is based on erroneous assumptions about the effectiveness of a proposed penalty or programme.

Given that restorative justice is a form of punishment, it is helpful to explore which philosophies of punishment are in evidence in restorative justice interventions. Studies have found that participants in restorative conferences bring to bear a mix of penal philosophies. In particular, retributive, restorative and rehabilitative principles and terms are intermingled in the interactions that take place. Indeed, successful restorative meetings provide evidence of a core sequence of shifts in penal focus. During initial discussions about the offence, including the harm it caused and the feelings it engendered, the principle most discernible is one of retributive censure. Subsequent discussions about making good the harms done turn the emphasis to restoration for the victim and other participants. This often includes, or progresses to, deliberations about the best ways of preventing reoffending, with a rehabilitation philosophy becoming germane. The progression, however, is not inevitable. If the victim or others perceive that retributive censure has failed to bring about acknowledgement of remorse by the offender, the shift to the reparative stage may not happen. In such cases participants may resort to deterrent or denigratory language and strategies in order to teach the apparently recalcitrant offender a lesson. Furthermore, victims are not likely to participate in discussions about offender rehabilitation and reintegration if their own losses have not been addressed adequately.

Restorative justice appeals to those who see benefits in allowing space for emotion in responses to crimes, but emotion mediated by civility. Emotion without deliberation can be a dangerous thing. Victim impact statements read out in court fall into this category. They give space for one-way emotional traffic, without the safeguards brought about by deliberation and, in particular, by deliberative accountability. For many, deliberative accountability is a fundamental principle of restorative justice.[45] All participants should have the chance to provide accounts of their own experiences, motivations and feelings about past behaviours, and should be allowed to articulate their aspirations. They should also feel empowered to challenge others' accounts and objectives, to ask for clarification or explanation when things are not clear, and to suggest when others might reassess their point of view. Within this process of deliberation and mutual accountability truths beyond evidential truths emerge, contexts are fully explored and the group can move towards consensus on what needs to be done to repair the harms.

Although most cases are likely to produce—through deliberative accountability—reparation agreements that are broadly speaking 'proportionate', checks are still necessary, especially in response to more serious crimes. Restorative justice and a more formal framework for proportionality do not have to be seen as incompatible. It is possible, and desirable, to have both. In order to avoid the pitfall of disproportionality, if not denigration, restorative agreements could be reached within a framework of upper and lower limits on the amount of reparation to which an offender should be liable, with discretion for the participants in each conference to choose not only the amount of reparation within these limits, but also the type of reparation.[46] That way the limits provide a safety

---

[45] This concept is developed by D Roche, *Accountability in Restorative Justice* (Oxford, Oxford University Press, 2003).

[46] This is the position adopted by M Cavadino and J Dignan, 'Reparation, Retribution and Rights' in A von Hirsch and A Ashworth (eds), *Principled Sentencing: Readings on Theory and Policy*, 2nd edn (Oxford, Oxford University Press, 1998).

net without constraining deliberative accountability in the process and the flexibility to decide on reparation that is meaningful to both victims and the wider community. They also provide a guide for those cases where reparation is in dispute.

When there is a difference of opinion about the amount of reparation, or the very need to make a reparative gesture, how should participants proceed? If the offender will not agree to what is thought by the other participants to be a fair and proportionate proposal for reparation, should the facilitator have the capacity to compel the offender both to agree to and then to honour that agreement? If restorative justice is the sentence that a court has imposed, such coercion may not be necessary. The facilitator could refer the case back to the court to consider if the original discounted tariff should be revised to take account of the failure of the conference to reach a fair reparation agreement. This would allow the court to increase the penalty either to what it would have been without a restorative conference, or to somewhere in between to reflect the offender's willingness to participate even though an agreement has not been reached. The danger here is that such recourse to the court would seem to undermine both the restorative process and the authority of those who participated in the process, but it might be the least undesirable option. In cases where an agreement has been made, but subsequently the participants express concern about its fairness, judicial oversight of reparation agreements could prevent a disproportionate agreement being carried through and give scope for revision of the agreement. This could be enforced by giving both victims and offenders the right of appeal to a court. Of course, if there are upper and lower limits this right of appeal is not likely to be exercised frequently. In diversionary conferences, where there is no court to which to refer the case, facilitators need a clear mandate for preventing disproportionate agreements (and the skills to facilitate the process of deliberation) but ultimately should not have the power to impose an agreement or coerce an offender.

Of course, proportionality is of concern not only to outcome agreements, but also to the restorative process. Restorative justice typically operates through mobilising pre-existing norms and discourses, seeking to hold offenders accountable and change their attitudes and behaviour. Participants expect offenders to talk about their feelings, to acknowledge harm to others, to listen to the views of fellow citizens about what they have done, and to apologise and make offers of restoration. Restorative dialogue clearly involves a form of moral disciplining, and most offenders find the experience fairly intrusive or uncomfortable, but it should not be denigratory and it should not seek to revictimise. Facilitators need to be alive to subtle forms of denigration, sometimes used against young offenders, and sometimes from their own supporters. Effective facilitation can help to prevent this by making clear at the start of the meeting the 'ground rules' for participation and then by maintaining the authority to impose these rules even when emotions run high, as they inevitably will.

The second group of restorative justice critics, referred to above, fear the introduction of restorative processes for anything but the most minor of crimes or offenders because of the potential for things to go wrong. They cite cases, actual or hypothetical (more often the latter), where power imbalances or unprofessional or ineffective facilitators derail the process, resulting in revictimisation or denigratory treatment of vulnerable offenders. Just as hard cases make for bad law, they make for premature or misguided rejection of a process, criminal or restorative.

The concerns of sceptics arise from failures of mutual accountability. It is inevitable in any genuinely participatory approach that on occasion things will fall apart, sometimes quite spectacularly. However, these hard cases represent a breakdown of program integrity, particularly of facilitation, rather than a collapse of the restorative ideals or philosophy. They signal a failure to deal effectively and sensitively with the worse side of human nature. Those harmed by offences, especially serious offences, are likely to be angry and might feel—initially at least—vindictive. They can be afraid and vulnerable, inarticulate or particularly voluble. They are, in other words, hurt people, often, remarkably, at their best, but sometimes at their worst.

Such victims can derail restorative processes. They might try to use the restorative encounter to denigrate rather than reintegrate offenders, to use the offence to try to show that the offender is a bad person, deserving of contempt and beyond redemption. They may also use various manoeuvres to produce reparation agreements that are degrading or overly harsh, rather than restorative. Restorative justice can, and should, cope with them. People should not be excluded from the process because they are 'too angry' or 'too contrite'. The facilitator should be able to negotiate these sometimes extreme, often conflicting emotions in order to accommodate deliberation and ultimately restoration and reparation.

Of course, mutual accountability can break down if one or more participants use their relative power or control to dominate proceedings or to excuse their own perspective. Offenders might seek refuge for their shame and discomfort by engaging in 'techniques of neutralisation', which, if left unchallenged, can undermine the restorative process. These techniques can involve offenders denying or underplaying the seriousness of their offence or their own culpability. Offenders might refuse to accept full responsibility by blaming others for their behaviour (they had no choice, or they were somehow forced to do it); or admit that they have broken the law but not that they have caused any real harm (the car was insured after all, or they stole from someone rich enough to absorb the loss); or assert that the victim is not deserving or legitimate (they acted in revenge or on an unworthy victim).[47] Such techniques can be managed within a restorative process where other participants feel able to challenge them or proffer alternative versions of the offender's perspective. A skilful facilitator can help them to do this by asking questions which encourage them to reflect and comment on the offender's version of events, and by scrutinising the offender's account. Indeed, restorative processes are particularly well placed for challenging techniques of neutralisation when they confront offenders with the results of their actions. It is much harder to

---

[47] G Sykes and D Matza, 'Techniques of Neutralization: A Theory of Delinquency' (1957) 22(6) *American Sociological Review* 664.

pretend that the victim was not really harmed, or that they some-how deserved to be offended against, when that very person is sitting opposite and making clear how he or she feels.

It might be instructive to pause here and reflect on the potential efficacy of restorative justice in responding to one of the most challenging of offences: hate crime. Homophobia, racism, disab-lism and other forms of prejudice mean that hate victims can feel extremely vulnerable, marginalised and disempowered by the dominant culture. Offenders and victims may live in different neighbourhoods, hold different beliefs and socialise in different groups. The social distance between them may mean that neither party can identify with the other's cultural backgrounds, and minority groups may be viewed with scepticism or as deserving of discrimination. Offenders may not be able to empathise with their victims, and victims' revelations might be perceived as provocative and elicit a hostile response from the offender. In such circum-stances ineffective facilitation by someone who does not fully understand the cultural tensions could fail to prevent repeat victimisation. Hate victims in such situations might feel compelled to accept disingenuous apologies in an attempt to appease the offender and reduce the likelihood of reprisals; and this, of course, is not the path to healing.

However, if managed sensitively and according to restorative principles, the process can diffuse conflict and expose ignorance and bigotry to critical scrutiny. Once prejudices are explored in a safe environment there is scope for effective challenge and subse-quent modification of perspectives. Defendants' racist or homo-phobic attitudes may not necessarily be deeply entrenched but could instead be the result of unthinking adoption of what is per-ceived at that time to be local consensus on immigration, for exam-ple. In the absence of evidence to the contrary, it may be easy to hold ignorant beliefs about 'outsiders', and to argue, erroneously, that such people threaten the status quo; but people's attitudes can change when they are confronted with an individual who seems, in many ways, similar to them. Indeed, a restorative conference may present the offender with his or her first opportunity to talk to a gay or a black person in a safe environment and, importantly, in the absence of provocation from others; and this may be enough to demonstrate that the prejudice is without merit.[48]

Clearly, whilst restorative processes might perpetuate existing power imbalances and inter-personal moral communication may engender counterproductive resentments, they have the potential to break down stereotypes and facilitate communication amongst people divided by ignorance and intolerance. The communitarian ideals behind restorative justice do not envisage the powerful imposing their will on others but, rather, values being formulated and reformulated by deliberation amongst all, and balancing areas of convergence with diversity. In practice, some conferences will fail to achieve deliberative consensus and will result in an agreement that reflects only the wishes of the most powerful. However, if restorative processes operate within a legal framework, with scope for legal checks and safeguards on reparation agreements, they are better able to avoid the dangers of the majority or the more powerful imposing unreasonable demands on the minority or the vulnerable. As for the hard cases, they challenge facilitation but not restorative justice theory, as is shown later in section VI.

4. Who should facilitate restorative processes?

Consideration of who should be invited to participate in restorative conferences, whether facilitators can coerce offenders and how they might persuade victims, or how they should manage proposals of disproportionate reparation or offenders reluctant to agree to any reparation, makes clear that the demands on a facilitator are considerable. Empirical research has shown that facilitators are crucial to the success of restorative processes, to ensuring that the practice follows restorative principles and that program integrity is maintained. So, who has the aptitude for facilitating restorative justice conferences?

---

[48] See further M A Walters and C Hoyle, 'Healing harms and engendering tolerance: the promise of restorative justice for hate crimes' in N Chakraborti (ed), *Hate Crime: Concepts, Policy, Future Directions* (Cullompton, Willan, 2010).

Restorative practices for all but non-criminal incidents, or the relatively minor cases deemed to be suitable for diversion from prosecution (for example as part of a cautioning scheme), should operate within the criminal justice system, with its attendant due process checks and balances, in order for their processes and outcomes to be restorative. However, this does not necessarily mean that criminal justice agents such as the police should facilitate restorative meetings. When restorative justice was first introduced into both Australia and the UK it was police-led, but more recently, in Australia in particular, criticisms of such practice have resulted in other professionals facilitating the process. It is crucial that facilitators are perceived by all involved to be both fair and impartial. They should have no *personal* agenda in deciding who participates or in the questions they ask of participants. It may not be realistic to expect professionals who are steeped in the adversarial and punitive system to take a key role in what is supposed to be a restorative process. Many regard the police as incapable of the kind of detachment required to ensure fair process. Police facilitation might well place too much power in their hands if they can investigate, arrest, judge and punish someone without sufficient legal safeguards against the abuse of these considerable powers. In particular, where the police are not considered to be legitimate, for example by certain marginalised communities, they should not perform central roles in restorative processes.

To consign restorative justice to agencies such as the police, whose primary roles and duties lie elsewhere, brings other risks too. The best intentions of those committed to restorative interventions struggle against limited resources and incompatible organisational goals. When governments demand a crackdown on street crime, restorative conferencing is likely to take a back seat, as was seen in the English Thames Valley Police service.[49] A better approach, both philosophically and pragmatically, would be the establishment of a specialist team of restorative justice facilitators.

---

[49] C Hoyle, 'Restorative Justice Policing in Thames Valley' (2009) 2(11) *Journal of Police Studies* 189 (Special Issue on Restorative Policing edited by L G Moor, T Peters, P Ponsaers and J Shapland).

Quasi-judicial facilitators, would, like stipendiary magistrates, bring independence to the process and have none of the cultural baggage or professional agendas of other state agents. They could serve the police or YOTs and, for more serious offences, the courts, probation services and the prisons by providing restorative conferences for referred cases. Such an agency would rapidly evolve experience and 'best practice', training and guidelines; and simply by virtue of the fact that its practitioners would be working full time on the facilitation of restorative justice processes, they could be expected not to exhibit the inappropriate interventions and departures from restorative philosophy seen at police-led conferences across the world. By definition independent, they might also be expected to command the authority and respect which some are wary of awarding to existing institutions, such as social workers and the police. Such a specialist cadre, fully trained and accredited, and accountable to and financed by statutory criminal justice agencies such as the police, the courts, probation and prisons, would signal the full maturation of restorative justice and its complete integration within the criminal process.

5. *Conclusion*

This section has made the case for protections and safeguards provided by the law. However, it is a call for us not to rely too much on the law and to use it sparingly. In order to do this, and not to disregard the needs of victims and communities harmed by crime and disorder, we need to look beyond the retributive to the restorative in those cases not sufficiently serious to require the intervention of the courts. In those cases where a financial, community or custodial penalty is necessary to meet the retributive needs of society, we need to use restorative processes to rebuild fragmented communities and heal damaged relations alongside a proportionately reduced retributive punishment. In this way—so long as it does not lead to net-widening—restorative justice could serve as a 'cooling device' to our current 'hot criminological climate' which seems determined to ratchet up sentencing and incarcerate greater numbers of offenders.[50] Further, in pursuing a complementary approach to punishment society need compromise neither its moral commitment to individual rights nor the good of the community and society more generally.

It is not worth establishing such a restorative justice agency and making a commitment to the spread of restorative justice practices to help the police deal only with shop theft or minor incidents of disorder; restorative justice should not be about freeing up criminal justice resources to concentrate on the big fish. If we acknowledge that restorative justice is a form of punishment, as well as a constructive means of engaging communities in the resolution of disputes and conflict, we should be prepared to utilise it across the criminal justice spectrum. Hence, section VI. below explores its potential in somewhat challenging circumstances, in responding to crimes considered by some to be beyond its reach. It concludes, however, by suggesting that while we should be braver about its use, there are some offences best responded to by pure retributivism.

VI. IN DEFENCE OF RESTORATION IN THE 'DEEP END' OF CRIMINAL JUSTICE

If restorative justice is about giving victims a voice, about empowering them to speak out about their experiences and seek reparation, why keep it only in the shallow end of criminal justice? By 'shallow end', I refer both to minor offences which have for a long time, in most jurisdictions, been the only crimes subject to restorative process (typically shop theft, theft of low-value property outside of homes or businesses, or minor disputes) and to less serious and less punitive sanctions, such as police cautions or conditional discharge from court. Conversely, the 'deep end' refers both to serious offences (typically assaults that cause injury or death, most sexual crimes and high-value fraud or property offences) and to punitive sanctions such as prison sentences.

---

[50] I Loader and R Sparks, *Doing Criminology in a Hot Climate*, paper presented to the American Society of Criminology Annual Meeting, Hyatt Hotel, St Louis, 11–15 November 2008.

Minor offences and disorder can cause considerable inconvenience to victims and create feelings of mistrust and resentment within communities, but it is the more serious crimes that bring about significant emotional harm both to individual victims and to the sense of safety of those within their community. Furthermore, as mentioned above, empirical research suggests that restorative justice—especially when used alongside retributive processes—is more likely to heal victims and deter reoffending when used for more serious crimes, especially crimes of violence, and for cases where there are personal victims.[51]

This is not to argue that restorative justice has no place in the shallow end, but rather that in such cases, parsimony should drive decision-making in order to avoid 'net-widening'. Restorative justice should be used for minor offence recidivists, who otherwise would likely find themselves with sentences that are increasingly punitive and disproportionate to the index offence. It should be used as a diversion from the criminal process in relatively minor cases where an informal police warning would seem inadequate, although the police need wider discretion to issue such brief, non-restorative warnings in very trivial cases with genuine first-time young offenders (as much as it is possible to know who really is a first-time offender, rather than a first-time *caught* offender). But it should also be used for more serious offences and offenders. At present, while New Zealand uses restorative processes for serious offences, those few cases that are disposed of using restorative practices in the UK are not serious, and yet there is some evidence that restorative justice can work with such cases. In 2001 the Home Office for England and Wales established a pilot study of three restorative justice schemes that, between them, covered restorative processes throughout all stages of the criminal process for adults and young people, serious and less serious offences. The pilot study was subject to rigorous academic scrutiny from a team of researchers at Sheffield University, whose reports demonstrate the efficacy of restorative justice, both in terms of reducing recidivism

---

[51] Sherman and Strang, above n 36.

and healing victims.[52] Despite these and other positive findings, there is relatively little in the way of restorative justice in the UK today, particularly for serious offenders.

There is some restorative work with hate crimes, although not for the most serious cases,[53] but almost none for serious assaults, robbery or homicide. Restorative processes should be used much more widely in the deep end of offending, for cases likely to have caused significant harm to victims and the wider community. However, within the deep end, controversies centre not only on offence seriousness but also on the relationship between victims and offenders. For this reason, this section will focus on two serious offences that have caused some enthusiastic supporters of restorative justice to recoil: crimes against humanity and domestic violence.

On initial consideration, it is far from obvious why the core restorative principles of respect, empowerment and dialogue should be applied to perpetrators of mass atrocities or to those who repeatedly and violently abuse their families. If we put aside consideration of the efficacy of restorative justice, which makes clear that it works best in serious cases, and take a normative position that it is fundamentally wrong to enter into any dialogue with the worst criminals, we are left only with the court system. Of course, even then there is a requirement to treat with dignity and respect those defending themselves against charges of genocide, for example.

A rejection of dialogic processes would be entirely appropriate if the suggestion was to provide civil mediation between victims

---

[52] J Shapland, A Atkinson, H Atkinson, B Chapman, E Colledge, J Dignan, M Howes, J Johnstone, G Robinson and A Sorsby, 'Restorative justice in practice: findings from the second stage of the evaluation of three schemes', *Home Office Research Findings 274* (London, Home Office, 2006); J Shapland, *Restorative justice: the views of victims and offenders* (London, Ministry of Justice, 2007); J Shapland, A Atkinson, H Atkinson, J Dignan, L Edwards, J Hibbert, M Howes, J Johnstone, G Robinson and A Sorsby, *Does restorative justice affect reconviction?: The fourth report from the evaluation of three schemes* (London, Ministry of Justice Research Series 10/08, 2008).

[53] Between 2007 and 2009, 144 hate incidents were referred for shuttle or direct mediation to the Hate Crimes Project, set up by the London Southwark Mediation Centre in 2000 (referrals are from statutory and third sector organisations, eg police, housing association, anti-social behavioural unit, victim support and self-referrals).

and perpetrators, as such processes are based on a presumption of equality between the parties. They start from a position of mutual respect and move towards resolutions that both parties find acceptable. Restorative justice is not conciliation. It unequivocally labels one party the wronged and the other the wrongdoer. It holds the latter accountable for his actions and tries to repair the harms caused to the former. Whilst it treats both parties respectfully and gives both parties the chance to tell their stories, it does not treat them equally; there is no moral equivalence.

Even so, objections may be made to the extension of restorative justice measures to serious crimes from the perspectives of both victims and society. Victims of serious offences might be at a greater risk of re-victimisation, especially when they have been specifically targeted and are vulnerable. The wider community, or society more generally, might not feel that reparative measures—even material reparation—are sufficient to condemn and deter most offenders. Reparatory gestures may be perceived as wholly insufficient to repair the harms caused by serious offences that have resulted in injury, death or significant mental suffering. Indeed, any such measure might be perceived to be insulting to the victims. Let us consider these objections by exploring one of the most intractable of social problems—domestic violence.

A. Domestic Violence[54]

Early feminist commentaries on domestic violence bemoaned the inadequate criminal justice response at a time when the police were

---

[54] This section draws on years of research into domestic violence; see, eg, C Hoyle, *Negotiating Domestic Violence: Police, Criminal Justice and Victims* (Oxford, Oxford University Press, 1998); C Hoyle and A Sanders, 'Police Response to Domestic Violence: from victim choice to victim empowerment?' (2000) 40 *British Journal of Criminology* 14; C Hoyle, 'Feminism, Victimology and Domestic Violence' in S Walklate (ed), *The Handbook of Victims and Victimology* (Cullompton, Willan, 2007). This section refers to offenders as males and victims as females. This is not to argue that this is always the case but to reflect the typical cases reported to the police. The dynamics of conferencing female domestic violence offenders may be different, but restorative justice could be equally useful in such relationships.

too often reluctant to intervene, dismissing domestic violence as a private or social service matter. Feminist agitation did much to persuade criminal justice agents to take seriously violence against women, and eventually a new orthodoxy emerged that 'taking seriously' meant arresting, prosecuting and punishing perpetrators. It also meant being clear who was the perpetrator and who the victim, and separating the two for as long as possible. However, just when their efforts have begun to bear punitive fruit, some feminist scholars are beginning to question the efficacy of prioritising retributive justice to the exclusion of other interventions.

The 'crime-centred' approach has been criticised for being paternalistic and limiting women's autonomy; for having an unequally negative impact on those who are already at increased risk of state interference (in particular, those with insecure immigration status or with a history of offending); and for being ineffective at ending abuse (empirical evidence shows that arrest and prosecution alone often fail to protect women and their children from further abuse). Victims know this, and even after significant improvements to the criminal justice system, including specialist domestic violence courts, many choose to retract their statements and withdraw their support for prosecution. Of course, their reluctance to cooperate with prosecution efforts is not just about the criminal justice system. There are many factors at work, including a genuine desire, on the part of the victim, to stay in the relationship. However, to date, the criminal process has failed to persuade a majority of victims of domestic violence that it can help them.

For those victims who are determined to leave a violent relationship and willing to testify against their perpetrators, the criminal process, in combination with other statutory and voluntary services of the type provided by Family Justice Centres, may be effective.[55] However, for those who are unsure or who are afraid to go to court, or for those whose decisions about the future are complicated by

---

[55] Family Justice Centres, currently being established in various US cities and in the London Borough of Croydon in the UK, bring together staff from law enforcement, forensic medical services, legal services and community-based organisations offering free services to all victims of domestic violence.

shared responsibilities for children, serious consideration should now be given to restorative approaches. Furthermore, for those of us who feel that the types of sanctions handed down by the courts are not likely to result in a reduction or cessation of domestic violence, restorative justice might hold some rehabilitative promise.

Restorative encounters may well be more likely than traditional criminal justice to hold offenders to account for their behaviour; to make possible a range of support services to victims; to result in reparation or compensation to victims (both symbolic and material); to mobilise both support for offenders and monitoring of their future behaviour; and to challenge patriarchal attitudes and normative judgements amongst offenders and their families or friends that excuse or condone physical or emotional abuse in particular and gendered domination more generally.

In many respects, feminism and restorative justice should not be uncomfortable bedfellows. They apparently share similar goals and values: a focus on choice and options; emphasis on personal empowerment; and rejection of the hierarchical, dichotomous and oppositional ways of doing justice. Truth telling and personal narratives are central to both philosophies. But *radical* feminism has locked horns with restorative justice. It has explicitly rejected the notion that victims' wishes should influence the statutory response to their victimisation and presumed, instead, to advocate in their *interests*, even though studies suggest that victims improve their chances of recovery when they play an active part in the response to the crime. In speaking out *for* victims, radical feminism has simultaneously denied those victims a voice. Restorative justice challenges this silencing of victims. Its raison d'être is to give victims a voice and a chance to participate fully in the state and community response to their victimisation.

Of course, there are pitfalls in using restorative justice for domestic violence, not the least of which concern the power and control perpetrators have over their victims. Restorative processes might perpetuate power imbalances if offenders are allowed to manipulate the informal process to diminish guilt, trivialise the violence, or shift the blame to the victim by engaging in techniques of neutralisation (see n 15). If the process permits power imbalances to go unchecked and reinforces abusive behaviour, it could reduce women's safety and put them at further risk of violence. It might be unrealistic to expect victims to be able to assert their own needs and promote their own interests in the presence of such perpetrators, especially if the offender's supporters are not challenging his viewpoint or, indeed, are condoning aggressive, controlling and sexist behaviours or attitudes. Under such conditions victims' participation could be disempowering and punitive, and they and even their supporters might be inhibited from telling the truth for fear of repercussions from the offender. Intimidated victims might accept derisory reparation offers in order to 'keep the peace' and no one may feel sufficiently empowered to challenge them. This may be particularly likely in some communities where the ideals of womanhood create a mindset that makes victims reluctant to advocate for themselves. Inexperienced or incompetent facilitators might mistake this for genuine consensus.

However, these risks are not absent in the criminal justice process. Many victims of domestic violence already feel disempowered and isolated by their partners' abusive and controlling behaviours, and the criminal justice system currently does little to eliminate this. Indeed, given that many become further disempowered by a justice system that is not supposed to consider their choices, it may be that restorative justice can provide an empowering forum for victims. Bringing friends, family and colleagues of the victim into the process, making them fully aware of the abuse, and encouraging them to look out for the victim in future, might provide sufficient support to reduce the risk of re-victimisation and enhance the victim's feelings of safety; more so than a fine or a court order. In particular, restorative processes that succeed in bringing together communities of support around victims may provide the best opportunity of ending their isolation, brought about by their abusers' controlling behaviours that too often drive away friends, family and other potential sources of comfort and assistance. Furthermore, restorative processes may be able to facilitate repair of the relationship, if this is what both parties want, and therefore might prove beneficial in cases where victims are currently unwilling to cooperate with a criminal prosecution because they genuinely do not wish to end the relationship. Of course, a restorative process that starts with thorough pre-conference consultation with both parties individually is much better placed than the criminal justice system for establishing the sincerity of complainants' assertions about reconciliation. Where victims want to end a violent relationship, a restorative conference may be able to provide the information and, more importantly, put in place the support networks to facilitate the separation.

Moreover, restorative justice would not be mandatory for victims of domestic violence, and would not necessitate total rejection of criminal justice and its protections. A purely restorative justice response to domestic violence could undermine reforms to the criminal justice system. If violent men were diverted from the courts and their offences dealt with by civil mediation, such as is used by family lawyers to negotiate the division of the matrimonial estate during divorce, it would clearly send out the wrong symbolic message about the seriousness of such offences. But this is not being advocated. In domestic violence cases where there has been an infraction of the criminal law, restorative justice should be imposed by a court. This provides clear and authoritative condemnation of the offender's behaviour and an expression—by the court and, by extension, society—of solidarity with the victim. The restorative intervention would be imposed in conjunction with a retributive or rehabilitative sentence, or as an alternative in less serious cases.

Restorative justice advocates, such as John Braithwaite, propose escalating responses to domestic violence, beginning with a restorative conference but with the ultimate possibility of imprisonment. Under this 'pyramid approach' to restorative and criminal justice, prison serves as a threat in cases where offenders do not change their behaviour. Although generally I am opposed to the pyramid approach, as it puts restorative justice in the role of the easy or light option for those who can be deterred and stops us treating like cases alike, I am sympathetic to it in the case of domestic violence, where repeat offences directly increase victimisation of one person or one family. Repeat chances for restorative justice in such cases put specific victims at significant further risk. This is not to say that a further opportunity for a restorative intervention is not appropriate but that where violence is frequently repeated, or becomes increasingly severe, other sanctions should be imposed either alongside or instead of a restorative meeting better to protect the victims.

Of course, it is possible for a court to impose a restorative sentence only if the offender has admitted guilt, or if victim has testified and there has been a guilty verdict. As mentioned above, many victims refuse to testify and—partly in consequence—many domestic violence perpetrators plead not guilty. If the victim refuses to testify having initially made a statement, the offer of a restorative conference—with no other penalty—in return for a guilty plea might provide the least bad outcome. In those cases where the victim refuses to cooperate with the criminal process and police and prosecutors do not consider the offence sufficiently serious to compel her to testify, a restorative conference might be an expedient form of diversion from prosecution. Better than the usual alternative of 'no further action'.

An integrated complementary response to domestic violence that empowers victims and censures but reintegrates offenders (especially those with children caught up in the dispute), within the framework of due process safeguards and standards, would be better able to reduce both the incidence and the effects of domestic abuse. It would increase the prospects of desistance or a reduction in violence, whilst making clear society's condemnation of domestic violence.[56] At times this would be more like restorative justice with safeguards and a greater focus on fair outcomes, but at other times it would look more like formal criminal justice with the ideals of reintegration securely embedded in the process. Either way, the instrumental and expressive functions would be better catered for than under the current criminal justice process.

---

[56] Barbara Hudson has described the potential of such an approach: B Hudson, 'Restorative Justice and Gendered Violence? Diversion or Effective Justice?' (2002) 42(3) *British Journal of Criminology* 616.

I have already discussed the potential of restorative justice for post-sentence sex offenders (see section IV.), but a word or two on its use in cases of homicide might help us to consider where, if at all, its limits lie. In North America, Mark Umbreit has used victim–offender mediation and restorative dialogue in cases of homicide.[57] His interventions demonstrated the potential of restorative justice, when used in addition to a retributive sentence (in these cases prison), to encourage offenders to consider fully the impact of their offences on secondary victims and to provide some answers for, and aid the recovery process of, those victims. In Australia successful conferences have also been facilitated by the charismatic restorative justice practitioner and advocate, Senior Sergeant Terry O'Connell.[58] So far so good, but in a handful of cases Umbreit exceeded the limits of restorative justice by facilitating sessions between families of murder victims and their killers, shortly before the murderers' executions. Although Umbreit has argued that this experience helped all concerned to achieve 'closure' and resolution—and it may well have—it is grotesque that any involvement with the state's taking of a further human life could be described as restorative. A re-integrative state execution is clearly a contradiction in terms.

B. Crimes against Humanity

While debate has raged amongst restorative justice proponents and detractors over the applicability of restorative principles and processes to serious domestic crimes such as violence, sexual assault and murder, restorative justice has materialised as a legitimate concept in international law and as a central objective of many transitional justice mechanisms addressing crimes against humanity. These

---

[57] M S Umbreit, W Bradshaw and R B Coates, 'Victims of Severe Violence Meet the Offender: Restorative Justice Through Dialogue' (1999) 6 *International Review of Victimology* 321; M Umbreit, *Second International Conference on Restorative Justice*, Fort Lauderdale, Fla, 7–9 November 1998.

[58] See the moving video, *Facing the Demons*, produced by 'Real Justice' at <http://www.iirp.org/books_n_videos.php>.

mechanisms include truth commissions (within some 18 or so post-conflict jurisdictions, many in South America but including the most famous example, the South African Truth and Reconciliation Commission); hybrid-traditional interventions (such as Rwanda's *gacaca* courts and Timor Leste's Community Reconciliation Processes); and other community-based reconciliation processes (such as the numerous reconciliation ceremonies that have taken place in post-conflict Bougainville in the South Pacific).[59]

There are, not surprisingly, staunch critics of restorative processes for those who commit crimes against humanity, although less so for the more general peace-building measures that take place under the umbrella of 'transitional justice mechanisms'. Retributivists, sometimes referred to within the transitional justice literature as 'legalists', believe that responding to war crimes, genocide or other crimes against humanity within the criminal justice framework, and in particular under the rules and jurisdiction of international criminal justice, is crucial to lasting peace, and that therefore all such cases should be subjected to international prosecution. Within this perspective, truth commissions and other measures broadly conceived of as restorative should be used only as a prelude to trials, and amnesties never contemplated. At the same time, many advocates of restorative justice believe that to be the only appropriate response to such offences, rejecting outright any form of retributive justice. These starkly contrasting and apparently entrenched viewpoints reflect, to some extent, the aforementioned dichotomous view of restorative and retributive justice (see section V.A.) and a failure to imagine a system that draws on both restoration and retribution.

Unlike most crimes, gross abuses of human rights cause harm not only to those directly victimised but also to their wider communities, leaving them feeling vulnerable, powerless and in need of collective, as well as individual, justice. At the micro level, there are

---

[59] J Braithwaite, H Charlesworth, P Reddy and L Dunn, 'Peacebuilding Compared, Working Paper 6, Bougainville, August 2009', downloaded from <http://peacebuilding. anu.edu.au/_documents/Workingpapers/BougainvilleWorkingPaperwebsitevers. pdf>.

individual victims and offenders, for whom restorative and retributive justice will both serve necessary but different purposes. At the macro level, fractured communities need both practical and symbolic help. Restoring the infrastructure and revealing the truth of what has happened will be important to healing the wounds of the past *and* to moving towards a functioning and cohesive society. A combination of international justice, national criminal justice and restorative justice may well be able to meet the needs of damaged communities at both the micro and macro levels.

International justice mechanisms can bridge the divide between these micro and macro needs. They can deal with individual victims and offenders. But by targeting those at the top of the chain of command, their symbolic message has a broader impact—not only for communities directly affected by the defendants' crimes, but also for those who may be thinking of perpetrating such crimes in future. International justice may go some way towards combating impunity through the act of prosecution, by securing public records and by creating international mechanisms to monitor the sometimes uneasy political truce and try to prevent further conflicts. By censuring the behaviour of perpetrators, the international courts acquire both a moral and a legal rationale, which meets the moral obligation to condemn. This is crucial, because with such offences it is not enough that perpetrators be asked to contribute to the reparative needs of those identified as specific victims; they must face retribution and censure from the entire international community. Retributive justice in the international arena also guarantees procedural and human rights safeguards, and due process protections for defendants that severely compromised nation states might not be able to provide (witness, for example, the public executions of those convicted of genocide in the aftermath of the Rwandan atrocities).

This is not to say that prosecutions will always, or even usually, bring an end to ongoing violence or deter future violence—indeed, there is an absence of robust empirical evidence that they have any such consequences—but that is not the aim of retribution. Retributive responses look back at crimes committed and censure them and punish them proportionately as an end in itself, not in order to bring about a consequentialist goal. It is for this reason that legal scholars who favour retribution on normative grounds consider empirical evidence about efficacy to be largely irrelevant.

At the level of the nation, the need is both to rebuild damaged infrastructures and to re-establish justice and equality before the law through trials, apology, documentation and the establishment of mechanisms to try to prevent a recurrence. International justice must not proceed at the expense of these mechanisms but alongside or preceding them; non-state alternatives should not be displaced by the liberal legalists' criminal justice, neither should they be the only option. To have any prospect of peace in the medium term, let alone long-term stability, societies need to make use of both retributive and restorative responses for theoretical, but also for pragmatic, reasons.

Let us consider the example of Rwanda. Following the genocide of 1994, Rwanda's prisons were overflowing and the criminal justice system almost ground to a halt. There were quite simply too many Hutu men awaiting trial for too long in intolerable conditions. Whilst the genocidaires became the responsibility of the International Criminal Tribunal for Rwanda, based in Tanzania, the vast majority of genocide suspects languished in worse conditions, faced the death penalty (until it was abolished in 2007) and were tried without adequate due process protections. The development of the traditional *gacaca* courts to deal with the less serious of these cases was not only an attempt to use restorative processes to involve victims and the community and try to heal the communal wounds caused by the genocide, but also a pragmatic way of taking the burden off the over-burdened criminal justice system. The *gacaca* courts provided a blend of reparation and retribution. Many defendants who took responsibility for their offences, making apologies and offers of reparation to their victims and their communities, escaped further punishment. Others avoided a return to prison by agreeing to do community service; but in some cases, in spite of this, they were sent back to prison by judges who deemed incarceration to be necessary to meet the needs of proportionality.

Gacaca courts—often described as 'restorative justice', but better seen as 'hybrid justice'[60]—clearly support the argument that punishment and reparation are not diametrically opposed, and both have their roles in transitional justice. But what of individual victims, or the surviving family members of those killed in conflicts? What are their needs, and how best can communities, including the international community, meet them?

There is, largely, consensus in the academic literature over what victims and communities need in the aftermath of large-scale conflict. Those harmed during conflicts and survivors who lost loved ones want recognition of their status as victims, specifically acknowledgement of the violation of their and their loved one's human rights, and a public record of the facts of what happened. They want these not only for material benefits such as compensation, but also for the symbolic value of recognition and to clear the ground for potential reconciliation. International justice can provide this acknowledgement, while establishing a documentary record of historical fact. This should provide some benefit to victims, even if their own individual experiences have not been acknowledged by the court.

In addition to public acknowledgement of their abuse, given the physical, material and psychological harm they have suffered victims generally require some form of reparation to restore their dignity, power and control, and to renew or strengthen their rights and citizenship. Reparations can be pivotal to a victim's and a community's recovery from crime, because they can help to repair damages done to the infrastructure and to the sense of safety of all citizens. They can acknowledge who was responsible for the devastation, and by doing so provide vindication to victims of the conflict. This may help to diminish victims' desire for revenge and therefore may reduce the chances for a potential escalation of the conflict. Reparation may be provided by compensation or restitution, as well as through rehabilitation and commemoration, including memorials to those who suffered or who tried to help the victims.

---

[60] See, eg, Clark, above n 10.

Historically, victims' rights have been relegated to a peripheral role by international criminal law and international humanitarian law. But recent years have seen the emergence of a growing international consensus that victims of human rights abuses are entitled to reparations, and that reparations play an important role in achieving justice for victims. For example, the International Criminal Court has gone much further to promote victims' participation than its predecessors, the *ad hoc* tribunals of Rwanda (ICTR) and the former Yugoslavia (ICTY). The recognition of the rights of victims both to participate in proceedings and to pursue reparations before the International Criminal Court represents a shift from the fundamentally retributive approach of the ICTY and ICTR to one in which retributive and restorative ideals coexist.

Restorative practices—in particular, reparation—are now becoming the foremost contemporary response in repairing societies torn apart by conflict. While they take a number of forms, they generally fall into two overlapping categories: material and symbolic reparation. Material reparations, such as financial compensation and restitution, though they can have strong symbolic meaning, generally address specific harms resulting from a crime. Symbolic reparations, such as apologies or memorials, attend to the harmfulness of acts themselves.

While financial reparations through national or international prosecutions have the potential to serve various restorative purposes, it should not be the intention of compensation to restore the status quo ante in full. For post-conflict societies to make the transition to peace, stability and restoration they also need truth telling, reconciliation, institutional reform and reparations beyond financial compensation and limited restitution. In some cases restoration and reintegration may only be possible following genuinely dialogic hybrid-restorative processes such as the Rwandan *gacaca* courts. These, and truth commissions, which can reveal narrative and dialogic truths, as well as evidential truths, operate at both the community and the individual level, and, as such, have the potential for full accountability. They also draw on both restorative and retributive philosophies.

The most celebrated truth commission—the South African Truth and Reconciliation Commission (SATRC)—was set up to re-establish the legitimacy of the state and the law, and to hold to account those responsible for state-sponsored discrimination and atrocities during almost five decades of apartheid. In seeking a peaceful transition to a viable democracy, and in needing to rely, at least in the short term, on the cooperation of some of those complicit in the horrors of the apartheid regime, the SATRC was necessarily the result of a compromise between retributive justice and a blanket amnesty, neither of which would have garnered the support of both of the opposing sides. Hence, South Africa witnessed the emergence of a partial 'truth for amnesty' compromise.

Like the Commissions in Argentina, Chile and Guatemala, the SATRC demonstrated that the work of truth commissions can be compatible with trials and punishments. The Amnesty Committee of the SATRC rejected some amnesty requests and urged the prosecution of those whom they judged to have withheld evidence or even lied, or who had gone further in their abuse and violation of citizens' rights than might have been expected in order to achieve their political aims—in other words, those who were disproportionately violent.[61] Similarly, criminal proceedings followed the publication of truth commission reports in Argentina and Chile. These were not, as some damning media reports would have us believe, blanket amnesties; defendants could not simply say sorry and be forgiven.

Some victims discovered truths in the SATRC: for some of those whose loved ones had 'disappeared' or been killed, the process uncovered historical or forensic truths about what had happened and when. But by giving a voice to victims, the process also provided them with the route to narrative truths, an opportunity to have their stories heard and their experiences validated. Inevitably, the overarching compromise sought by the process resulted in some victims feeling that their search for subjective narrative

---

[61] For an authoritative discussion of the pros and cons of the SATRC, see various essays in R I Rotberg and D Thompson, *Truth v Justice: The Morality of Truth Commissions* (Princeton, Princeton University Press, 2000).

truths was undermined by the Commission's quest to establish factual truths. Nonetheless, most historians have declared the SATRC to have been a success, for those who gave evidence, for those who were held accountable and for the country as a whole. It did not provide a great deal in the way of reparation, either material or symbolic, and it did not fully heal the wounds inflicted over almost five decades of state-sponsored abuse. However, it did facilitate the establishment of a functioning democracy, with a new constitution, and it did give a voice to at least some of the victims. In this sense, it empowered both individuals and the nation.

Of course, this is not to argue that truth commissions will always bring about reconciliation, or will always be appropriate for conflict-torn communities. Truth commissions can be incongruent with local ways of coping. Some cultures prefer to remain silent, to get on with their lives and try to forget. Nevertheless, restorative processes that are sensitive to local contexts can take account of cultural differences and accommodate them, at least to some extent; they can be part of the development of grassroots practices of social recovery. The most symbolic of reparations is an apology, and apologies are much more likely to result from dialogic restorative justice processes, or from truth commissions, which are also more likely to result in public apologies or apologies from bystanders whose failure to act contributed in an indirect way to the harms caused to the victims.

However societies torn apart by crimes against humanity choose to respond to the perpetrators, the response will likely be a compromise, with the inevitable disconnect between victims' needs and the needs of the state. However, there is in most cases a strong case for drawing on both restoration and retribution. Having experienced extreme lawlessness, victims and survivors need to be reintegrated into a community where they can once again feel protected by the law. The law needs to reassert its legitimacy—a task that requires a measure of retributive justice—but this needs to be accompanied or followed by restorative practices in order to achieve a sustainable peace. Neither 'top-down' nor 'bottom-up' processes are sufficient alone to meet victimised communities' micro and macro needs, while the wider international community also needs to see justice done and the denunciation and punishment of atrocious deeds.

C. Everything has its Limits

It might be thought that an argument for using restorative practices in response to genocide leads to the conclusion that nothing is beyond the reach of restorative justice. However, I am not arguing for restorative measures to be used in response to all crimes, and certainly not to all crimes against humanity. There are certain preconditions that should be met before restoration and reintegration are contemplated. Those who steal a motor car or assault a rival fan at a football game must admit their guilt and be prepared to speak openly and honestly about their offence before the victim and wider community should even consider reintegration. Similarly, those who commit the worst atrocities must have stopped offending, and be willing to change and to help, in both the short and the long term, to rebuild a less divisive and safe community. It is not necessary that they be at the stage of pouring out their heart and begging for forgiveness, because this is a potential outcome, rather than a precondition, of restorative justice. Yet they must at the very least be prepared to acknowledge that what they have done was wrong and has caused considerable harm.

Contemporary Zimbabwe provides a good example of a country not ready for restorative justice. In the summer of 2009, the new 'Unity' Government launched a debate about 'national healing' after years of severe political violence and abhorrent state crimes committed by Robert Mugabe's Zanu (PF) Party, and unveiled the 'Organ for National Healing, Reconciliation and Integration'. The Prime Minister, Morgan Tsvangirai, made clear that those found responsible for atrocities, including murder, rape and torture, should 'not necessarily' be sent to jail.[62] Drawing on the messages of restorative justice, he stressed that he was 'not just saying—

---

[62] *BBC News*, 30 July 2009.

forgive, heal and reconcile', but that 'justice needs forgiveness . . . and if we do retributive justice, the danger is that we may slide back' towards violence. Not surprisingly, some of the victims have expressed concern they will not see justice or compensation. One man who is still being taunted and threatened by those who killed his wife and destroyed his home made clear that 'it is very difficult to forgive people who are still boasting about it.'

Zimbabwe is clearly in a very different place from post-apartheid South Africa, and while there have been changes, their future security remains uncertain. The Government's attempts to introduce reconciliatory processes demonstrate a cynical strategy to stay beyond the reach of international justice. Restoration might have a role in the future of Zimbabwe, but only once the country has a truly democratic government, elected following fair and accountable election procedures, and only once those responsible for the atrocities have acknowledged their guilt and paid a price for their crimes. In other words, in such a jurisdiction, retribution may well be a necessary precondition for restoration. As one of the coordinators of the Catholic Commission for Justice and Peace in Zimbabwe put it:

> I fear [the government] may go for a process of blanket amnesty, call it a time of madness and say let bygones be bygones, . . . If that happens, there is never going to be a time that we can have another election without bloodshed.[63]

There has been recent interest in the potential of restorative processes for victims of sexual violence, whether in the home or at the hands of strangers. A few adult victims of such violence might be able to benefit from restorative approaches if used in addition to retributive sentences, or as an alternative in very minor cases, and, as described in section IV. above, circles of support and accountability offer a promising restorative solution post-sentence. However, restorative conferencing for child victims of serious sexual or violent assault would be intolerable. Restorative justice requires dialogue; it relies on deliberative accountability, without which it ceases

---

[63] *The Times*, 17 April 2009, at 34.

to be restorative. Whilst other participants drawn from the community of support around the victim, or the wider community, can discuss the harms done and the best approach to reparation, the victim must have some involvement in this process. As we have seen, this does not necessarily mean that they have to face the offender, but it does mean that they have to be able and prepared to articulate their experiences, their feelings and their aspirations, and be able to consider and respond to the offender's story. Child victims of serious offences cannot be expected to participate in full. They are vulnerable and without sufficient power. They may remain under the control of manipulative offenders who may well be insufficiently empathetic to engage fully with the restorative process. For these reasons, and others, restorative conferences should not be available in cases of child sexual abuse, even as a supplement to retributive punishments.

VII. CONCLUSION: RESTORATION FOR FRAGMENTED COMMUNITIES

Restorative justice provides opportunities for communication and apology, two things that people in postmodern societies are in danger of forgetting how to do. In a world where virtual communication is increasingly replacing face-to-face conversations, and where misdeeds are met with defensive stances on the one side and litigious intent on the other, some with a more communitarian bent lament the lost art of explanation, consideration, apology and reintegration. Consequently we are pleasantly surprised by reparative and reintegrative gestures in response to conflicts which too often escalate into entrenched disputes.

Recently the world's media were bowled over by the results of a meeting convened at the White House by the US President, Barack Obama, which could be described as restorative. It was an apparently successful attempt to use face-to-face communication to defuse a situation which otherwise might all too easily have produced a bitter adversarial conflict. His guests were the African-

American Harvard professor Henry Louis Gates and Sergeant Jim Crowley, the white police officer who had arrested him in his own home, after a neighbour called 911 and claimed he was breaking in. Gates was held for disorderly conduct after accusing the officer of racism, and his arrest swiftly reignited the debate about the treatment of ethnic minorities by criminal justice agents in America.

The incident was already dominating the US media, and as both sides took up what looked like entrenched positions, it threatened to spiral out of control. Had it done so, it might well have negated the considerable progress Obama had already made in removing some of the bitterness from America's ongoing racial conundrum, and abruptly have closed the new chapter of white–black relations opened by his election. Obama's solution was to invite both the professor and the officer, along with Vice-President Joe Biden, to the Rose Garden for a beer. Although reports stated that no one apologised, Sergeant Crowley later told reporters that he and Professor Gates 'agreed to move forward' and use the opportunity 'to foster greater sympathy among the American public for the daily perils of policing on the one hand, and for the genuine fears of racial profiling on the other hand'.[64] For his part, Gates said that he and the officer 'hit it off right from the very beginning. When he's not arresting you, Sergeant Crowley is a really likable guy.'[65]

President Obama summed up the meeting as

> an attempt to have some personal interaction when an issue has become so hyped and so symbolic that you lose sight of just the fact that these are people involved, including myself, all of whom are imperfect.[66]

It was soon evident that these aspirations had been met. An affair that might have rumbled on for months, poisoning the nation's discourse, simply dropped out of both the news and the legal process. Instead of nursing their respective grievances, Gates and Crowley

---

[64] *BBC News*, 31 July 2009.
[65] *New York Times*, The Caucus blog, 31 July 2009, <http://thecaucus.blogs.nytimes. com/2009/07/31/gates-reflects-on-beers-at-the-white-house/?hp>.
[66] *Ibid.*

appeared to have acquired a sense of closure, and were able to get on with their lives.

The crimes and harms that attract interventions from the police and other criminal justice agents do not usually take place on such a public stage, and the supporters who show up at a restorative conference will be much less numerous than the millions who might, had the Crowley–Gates conflict continued to deepen, have felt involved or wronged. However, there are some relevant parallels. Like Professor Gates's arrest, many crimes consist of brief and sudden events that have the capacity to change the lives of both victims and offenders irrevocably. Some of the harms they cause may well be irreparable. Yet the challenge for society is to devise means that tend to reduce or heal the damage, while also giving perpetrators a way back from the brink—a route towards their re-acceptance as members of the community.

The adversarial criminal process is not very good at achieving these ends. As we have seen, it often leaves victims feeling disempowered, re-victimised and forced to deal with a new source of grievance. Meanwhile, traditional methods of punishment, especially imprisonment, often deepen the gulf between offenders and their community, worsening their sense of alienation and increasing the likelihood that they will reoffend. Over the years, a variety of methods to lessen these drawbacks has been tried and put into effect, from victim impact statements and counselling to cognitive-behavioural courses in prison. But however valuable these may sometimes be, they all essentially skirt the central problem—the vexed and complex interaction between community, victim and offender. In the very different arenas in which they may be applied, from cases of pre-teen shoplifting to crimes against humanity, restorative processes can provide a way to address this. There is now compelling empirical evidence that, done right, they can 'work' and that, like Gates and Crowley, and indeed President Obama, their protagonists can emerge from such processes in a better state of mental, emotional and 'social' health than would otherwise have been the case.

The tragedy of restorative justice over the past 15 years is that it has become a victim of some of its own advocates' rhetoric, a casualty of the over-inflated claims and expectations they raised. Swept away by their enthusiasm for its evident potential, it was they who erected the false dichotomy between restorative and criminal justice, apparently convinced that once the advantages of restorative justice became obvious to all, traditional processes would simply wither away. In hindsight, their optimism looks as naive as that once held by certain species of Marxist, who believed that establishing 'really existing socialism' would soon lead to the withering away of the state. But by arguing in such terms, they inadvertently did the restorative cause grave damage. They claimed, for example, that restorative justice would dramatically cut reoffending rates. When it began to be apparent that it did not, it was easy for politicians, police officers and others juggling tight public budgets to disregard its other possible benefits. The false dichotomy opened the way to further, crushing critiques, such as the concerns raised over disproportionality and due process. Had supporters of restorative justice not presented the choice between restorative and criminal justice in such stark, 'either/or' terms, restorative processes would have been much easier to defend, and this more than anything explains why, as we have seen, restorative justice is now so much studied but seldom practised.

The early, 'maximalist' advocates of restorative justice were naive and incautious. On the other hand, it is also easy to see why they got so carried away—because restorative justice and restorative processes *do* offer possible solutions to problems that have become more intractable than ever. The challenge is to deploy them in the most appropriate way, without illusions as to their capabilities. Moving beyond that crude, false dichotomy, we need to review the use of restorative justice and to see it as a continuum. There will indeed be circumstances where a pure restorative conference, as long envisaged by restorative justice's most evangelical choir, will on its own provide the best route to an outcome considered just by all concerned. On other occasions, it should be seen as an important but subordinate adjunct to the 'normal' criminal process. This, however, does not diminish its value.

We need to conduct this debate urgently if restorative justice is to survive, for I get the sense that it is currently on a knife edge, and that its future—if it has one at all—is likely to be determined relatively soon. One possibility is that restorative justice will shortly stop being used altogether, and that both it and its vast literature will soon be consigned to the status of historical footnotes—baffling curios to be disinterred by criminal justice researchers from the centuries to come.

There is, of course, an alternative. It is possible to envisage restorative processes that work in tandem with the courts, police and prisons; that pay full regard to due process and human rights; that are subject to external invigilation. It is possible to advocate the much more widespread use of such processes without referring to crude measures such as reoffending rates, and to see that they may have the capacity to heal where conventional responses have often seemed almost futile, such as in some cases of domestic violence.

Above all, restorative justice can provide means not only to resolve conflicts between victims and offenders, but also, through the very act of participation, to recast communities and reverse the process of their atomisation, whether this has been caused by the computerised retreat from face-to-face discourse or by fears of rampant anti-social behaviour and crime. This is too great a prize to ignore. Those, like me, who see the potential of restorative justice, need to reformulate its case, and to make it loudly, in the most public ways.

BIBLIOGRAPHY

New students of restorative justice will find many edited collections and readers to introduce them to the key debates and the influential writers in this field (see, for example, D Sullivan and L Tifft (eds), *Handbook of Restorative Justice* (Abingdon, Routledge, 2008); G Johnstone and D Van Ness (eds), *Handbook of Restorative Justice* (Cullompton, Willan, 2007); and C Hoyle (ed), *Restorative Justice* (Abingdon, Routledge, 2010)). Understanding of the subject will be enhanced by a close reading of the enormously influential writings of John Braithwaite, starting with his seminal text, *Crime Shame and Reintegration* (Cambridge, Cambridge University Press, 1989), and *Restorative Justice and Responsive Regulation* (Oxford, Oxford University Press, 2002). Anthony Bottoms provides a meticulous sociological analysis of the rise of restorative justice and its place in modern penality in 'Some Sociological Reflections on Criminal Justice' in A von Hirsch, J Roberts, A E Bottoms, K Roach and M Schiff (eds), *Restorative Justice and Criminal Justice: Competing or Reconcilable Paradigms?* (Oxford, Hart Publishing, 2003). Kathy Daly's extensive empirical and theoretical work provides a sober check on the early, aspirational literature (K Daly, 'Restorative Justice: The Real Story' (2002) 4(1) *Punishment and Society* 55; 'Mind the Gap: Restorative Justice in Theory and Practice' in A von Hirsch, J Roberts, A E Bottoms, K Roach and M Schiff (eds) *Restorative Justice and Criminal Justice: Competing or Reconcilable Paradigms?* (Oxford, Hart Publishing, 2003)).

Evidence of the potential of restorative justice to restore victims is found in the work of James Dignan (*Understanding Victims and Restorative Justice* (Maidenhead, Open University Press, 2005), especially pp 132–61) and in the empirical work of Heather Strang and Lawrence Sherman ('Repairing the Harm: Victims and Restorative Justice' (2003) 1 *Utah Law Review* 15). Daly's work shows, however, that the impact on victims is variable and mediated by a range of external factors (K Daly, 'The Limits of Restorative Justice' in D Sullivan and L Tifft (eds), *Handbook of Restorative Justice* (Abingdon, Routledge, 2008)). The work of George Pavlich (*Governing Paradoxes of Restorative Justice* (London, Glasshouse Press, 2005)) provides a theoretically informed critique of restorative justice. He argues we need to re-think some of the basic concepts of crime, victim, offender and community if restorative justice is to fulfil its promise as an alternative to state approaches.

For an interesting discussion of its role in rebuilding communities the reader can turn to K McEvoy and H Mika, 'Punishment, Policing and Praxis: Restorative Justice and Non-violent Alternatives to Paramilitary Punishments in Northern Ireland' (2001) 11 *Policing and*

Society 359 (although Robert Weisberg alerts us to the danger of exclusive and punitive communities: 'Restorative Justice and the Danger of "Community"' (2003) 1 *Utah Law Review* 343). Adam Crawford's critical examination of communitarianism and the role of restorative justice in healing communities is particularly instructive: see A Crawford, 'Appeals to Community and Crime Prevention' (1995) 22 *Crime, Law and Social Change* 97; A Crawford, 'Joined-up but fragmented: Contradiction, ambiguity and ambivalence at the heart of New Labour's "Third Way"' in R Matthews and J Pitts (eds), *Crime, Disorder and Community Safety: A new agenda?* (London, Routledge, 2001). His chapter, 'The State, Community and Restorative Justice: Heresy, Nostalgia and Butterfly Collecting' in L Walgrave (ed), *Restorative Justice and the Law* (Cullompton, Willan, 2002), explores the potential for a constructive relationship between communities and the state, with both sides correcting the excesses of the other. Rather than dismissing the state, as some restorativists do, Crawford argues that it has a crucial task in mitigating the inequities and potential for abusing power that are present within most communities, as well as creating the conditions for public participation in deliberative justice.

As proponents of a desert-based justification for sentencing, Andrew Ashworth and Andrew von Hirsch have consistently expressed concerns about restorative justice, especially the potential for disproportionate outcomes. At times this has taken the form of an academic debate between them and John Braithwaite and Philip Pettit, in response to a book published in 1990 by Braithwaite and Pettit called *Not Just Deserts: A Republican Theory of Criminal Justice* (Oxford, Clarendon Press, 1990) (see A von Hirsch and A Ashworth, 'Not Not Just Deserts: A Response to Braithwaite and Pettit' (1992) 12(1) *Oxford Journal of Legal Studies* 83; and P Pettit with J Braithwaite, 'Not Just Deserts, Even in Sentencing' (1992) 4(3) *Current Issues in Criminal Justice* 225). Their philosophical objections to restorative justice, and in particular to the enhanced role of victims and the community in deciding appropriate sentences, are further developed in A von Hirsch, A Ashworth and C Shearing, 'Specifying Aims and Limits for

Restorative Justice: A 'Making Amends' Model?' in A von Hirsch, J Roberts, A Bottoms, K Roach and M Schiff (eds), *Restorative Justice and Criminal Justice: Competing or Reconcilable Paradigms?* (Oxford, Hart Publishing, 2003), where they suggest a model of restorative justice that might be acceptable from a rights-based perspective. This is an interesting edited collection that shows how the field of restorative justice has matured, with those for and against now engaging in reasoned debates about potentials and pitfalls.

Nonetheless, the issue of proportionality has not yet been resolved, despite Michael Cavadino and James Dignan's proposal of a compromise whereby participants in restorative conferences can make reparation agreements within prescribed upper and lower limits: 'Reparation, Retribution and Rights' (1997) 4 *International Review of Victimology* 233. And some persist in the view that restorative justice and proportionality are incompatible concepts anyway (J Braithwaite, 'In Search of Restorative Jurisprudence' in L Walgrave (ed), *Restorative Justice and the Law* (Cullompton, Willan, 2002)).

Much of the discussion in the recent literature on restorative justice has focused on the question of whether and to what extent it is a punishment. In a series of papers, Kathy Daly has put forward persuasive arguments that restorative justice includes elements of punishment (eg 'Revisiting the Relationship between Retributive and Restorative Justice' in H Strang and J Braithwaite (eds), *Restorative Justice: Philosophy to Practice* (Aldershot, Ashgate, 2000)), whilst Lode Walgrave has been equally resolute that restorative justice and punishment are conceptually distinct ('Imposing Restoration and Inflicting Pain' in A von Hirsch, J Roberts, A E Bottoms, K Roach and M Schiff (eds), *Restorative Justice and Criminal Justice: Competing or Reconcilable Paradigms?* (Oxford, Hart Publishing, 2003)).

Over the last decade, those for and against the expansion of restorative justice have debated its role in responding to 'difficult' offences such as domestic violence and sexual assault (see B Hudson, 'Restorative Justice and Gendered Violence: Diversion or Effective Justice?' (2002) 42(3) *British Journal of Criminology* 616;

J Stubbs, 'Beyond apology? Domestic Violence and Critical Questions for Restorative Justice' (2007) 7(2) *Criminology and Criminal Justice* 169; D Coker, 'Transformative Justice: Antisubordination Processes in Cases of Domestic Violence' in H Strang and J Braithwaite (eds), *Restorative Justice and Family Violence* (Cambridge, Cambridge University Press, 2002); K Daly, 'Restorative Justice and Sexual Assault: An Archival Study of Court and Conference Cases' (2006) 46(2) *British Journal of Criminology* 334; and A Cossins, 'Restorative Justice and Child Sex Offences: The Theory and the Practice' (2008) 48 *British Journal of Criminology* 359). A discussion of research findings on mediation in cases of serious violence is provided by M Umbreit, W Bradshaw and R Coates, 'Victims of severe violence in dialogue with the offender: key principles, practices, outcomes and implications' in E Weitekamp and H-J Kerner (eds), *Restorative Justice: Theoretical Foundations* (Cullompton, Willan, 2002); and M Umbreit and B Vos, 'Homicide Survivors Meet the Offender Prior to Execution: Restorative Justice Through Dialogue' (2000) 4(1) *Homicide Studies* 63; whilst a critique of such practices can be found in M Radelet and M Borg, 'Comment on Umbreit and Vos' (2000) 4(1) *Homicide Studies* 88.

Criminologists and sociologists have only recently considered the potential of restorative justice in responses to crimes against humanity. In approaching this new field they would benefit from in-depth critical studies of current responses to conflicts. The field of political science is rich in such accounts, and recent articles by Phil Clark and Lars Waldorf, both of whom have spent long periods of time in Rwanda interviewing those who were involved in the genocide and those who have experienced the *gacaca* process, provide us with persuasive arguments for and against the use of restorative practices: L Waldorf, 'Mass Justice for Mass Atrocity: Rethinking Local Justice as Transitional Justice' (2006) 79 *Temple Law Review* 1; and P Clark, 'The Rules (and Politics) of Engagement: The Gacaca courts and post-genocide justice, healing and reconciliation in Rwanda' in C Hoyle (ed), *Restorative Justice* (Abingdon, Routledge, 2010). And for an authoritative account of the South African Truth and Reconciliation Commission, see the collection of essays in R I Rotberg and D Thompson (eds), *Truth v Justice: The Morality of Truth Commissions* (Princeton, NJ, Princeton University Press, 2000). Critical literature in this area questions whether a 'top-down' restorative justice approach is counterproductive to ensuring democratisation and participation (P Lundy and M McGovern, 'The Role of Community in Transitional Justice' in K McEvoy and L McGregor (eds), *Transitional Justice From Below: Grassroots Activism and the Struggle for Change* (Portland and Oxford, Hart Publishing, 2008); and O Lin, 'Demythologizing Restorative Justice: South Africa's Truth and Reconciliation Commission and Rwanda's Gacaca Courts in Context' (2006) 12 *ILSA Journal of International and Comparative Law* 41). Similarly, Blagg has argued that restorative justice has not satisfied indigenous demands for greater control over the development and operation of local justice mechanisms (H Blagg, *Crime, Aboriginality and the Decolonization of Justice* (Annandale, Hawkins Press, 2008)).

The Limitations of Restorative Justice

I. INTRODUCTION

A S I SAT DOWN to begin writing this essay, it was difficult not to feel overwhelmed by the volume of literature surrounding restorative justice. My research assistant had come back to me after a couple of weeks working on various databases, with 146 pages of references to material covering everything from school bullying to genocide, spanning the globe from New Zealand to Northern Ireland, from Singapore to South Carolina. My assistant e-mailed me to say she was worried there were thousands of documents she had missed—the restorativejustice.org online library alone referred to over 9,000 publications. The invitation to write this essay included a requirement to provide a 'fresh, original and provocative statement'. Being provocative with restorative justice may be relatively easy; being fresh and original is a much harder task.

In some respects it is passé to refer to the size of the restorative justice industry and its burgeoning literature, yet the magnitude and heterogeneity of the literature makes the task of description, analysis and critique more difficult. There is no single story of restorative justice. There are diverse practices and multiple layers of explanation and theory. Restorative justice covers a range of practices that might occur at various points within the criminal justice process, including pre-court diversion, processes working in conjunction with the court including at the point of sentencing, and post-sentencing with prisoners. It may include juvenile offenders, or adult offenders or both. We can see examples of restorative justice in victim–offender mediation, in family group and youth justice conferencing, and in sentencing circles. We can also see claims to restorative justice as a principle in post-conflict and transitional justice settings such as the South African Truth and Reconciliation Commission. In addition there is a range of areas outside the criminal law where restorative justice practices have been used, including workplaces, schools and child protection.

Despite the multiplicity of practices, many would argue that there are core elements which need to be satisfied to 'fit' within a restorative justice paradigm. Restorative justice can be defined in a number of ways—as a process, for instance, or as a set of values or goals, or more broadly as a social movement seeking specific change in the way criminal justice systems operate. A frequently cited definition is that restorative justice 'is a process whereby parties with a stake in a specific offence collectively resolve how to deal with the aftermath of the offence and its implications for the future'.[1] This definition emphasises the process requirement that all parties have an opportunity to be heard about the consequences of the crime and what needs to be done to restore victims, offenders and the community. Other definitions emphasise the values and goals of restorative justice rather than the process. The core values are said to be healing relationships between all parties involved, community deliberation rather than state-centred control of decision-making, and non-domination.

This essay reflects a deep ambivalence about restorative justice. At the same time the essay was being developed my 5-year-old son started school. On his first day he and I attended the office of our local state primary school. At the office entrance was a sign headed 'Restorative Justice', which set out a list of principles which the school followed. The logo on the bottom of the sign was *Real Justice*—a registered name of a company promoting restorative justice in Australia, North America and Europe. It caused me to reflect momentarily on the transnational trade in restorative justice. The development, the appeal and the policy transfer of restorative

---

[1]   T Marshall, *Restorative Justice An Overview* (London, Home Office, 1999) 5.

justice all have a significant transnational dimension. Restorative justice is an international business. But I also reflected briefly on my own early education at a local Catholic school where, rather than a set of restorative justice principles, there was a rack containing an assortment of canes for physically disciplining children. It is hard to oppose restorative justice as a set of normative principles preferable to a 'just deserts' model of punishment. But, as I will argue in this essay, the ambivalence towards restorative justice arises from the great expectations which are placed upon the normative framework it promises, and the reality of limited, fragmented and ambiguous change which has actually occurred as a result of restorative justice programs.

What I set out to do in this essay is to present one story of restorative justice: a critique that highlights what I see to be the major limitations of restorative justice theory and practice. But before I outline my concerns with restorative justice, I must acknowledge that in its more critical manifestations, restorative justice theory *may* provide a critique of key conceptualisations and institutions of the criminal justice system. It has the (largely unrealised) potential to challenge the discourses of criminalisation and punishment if it adopts a reflexive position about its own development and current place in relation to state power. It has the potential to decentre the notion of 'crime' to the extent that categories of 'harm', 'conflict' and 'dispute' replace the state's exclusive definition of criminal behaviour; yet this is a potential which has not been realised, as restorative justice has generally suffered incorporation into existing criminal justice systems. Restorative justice can also provide an opportunity to rethink the relationship between victim, offender and community, and in particular challenge the idea that the rights and interests of the victim and offender are diametrically opposed in a 'zero sum' relationship. A movement away from the zero sum thinking that pervades public discussions on penality would in itself be a great achievement.

One part of the story of restorative justice has been the search for legitimacy through establishing what Kathy Daly has called restorative justice's 'myths of origin': origins which are said to lie in pre-state societies or indigenous communities, or, in the modern period, in a concern for victim's rights and informal justice.[2] I shall return to this question in due course. For now I simply make the point that the narratives about restorative justice are shrouded in various claims which fail to provide a more critical appreciation of why restorative justice emerges at a particular time and with what effect. One task I have set in this essay is to explore the question of why restorative justice has appeared at this specific historical juncture, and why it has received such apparently widespread acceptance.

One of the major theoretical problems underpinning restorative justice is the claim to universalism. The attempt to establish its ethical superiority rests on what I see as an untenable claim to the universal good which restorative justice is said to deliver. This universalism reaches down into the very notions of 'offender' and 'victim', which are seen as essentialist categories devoid of particular social characteristics and identities. Paraphrasing Pashukanis' critique of bourgeois legal categories, restorative justice seeks to 'universalise and materialise' legal subjects with certain attributes of individual responsibility, accountability and civic obligation. Unless restorative justice can establish universal attributes for all offenders and victims, it faces the risk that its own particular processes of bringing the offender and victim together, and its epistemological claims of establishing a superior truth to that provided by traditional court processes, will be seen simply as an alternative way of dealing with criminal behaviour without any particular foundational claim to legitimacy. The universal pretensions of restorative justice underpin its claim to legitimacy as a normative theory.

An entrenched assumption in restorative justice is that it is an ethically preferred model of doing justice: it is an inherently *good thing* to do. The problem this poses is that it is difficult to argue the limitations of restorative justice without being seen as an apologist for more retributivist or punitive approaches to criminal justice. Yet this simple dichotomising between restorative and retributivist

---

[2] K Daly, 'Restorative Justice: The Real Story' (2002) 4 *Punishment and Society* 55.

justice, between state and non-state justice is part of the problem. It simplifies what is in reality a highly complex set of social, political and cultural relations in which justice and particularly punishment are embedded. The dichotomy drawn by restorative justice between state and civil society makes it more difficult to understand how the law operates through civil society; or more particularly how restorative justice is caught within the networks of power and law that permeate social life. The institutions of civil society are continually constituted and reconstituted through the laws, policies and practices which the state puts in place.

Virtually everyone writing in the area appears to believe that restorative justice is beneficial—it is presented as a commonsense approach to doing justice that respects victims and offenders, and returns the problem of crime to the community. It takes a social problem away from the state and its impersonal, bureaucratic processes of dealing with human conflict and pain, and returns it to those most affected. In Nils Christie's famous conceptualisation, 'conflict' as a property is returned to the community.[3] Even the fact that many academics and practitioners writing about restorative justice refer to it by the acronym of 'rj' gives it a kind of folksy, feel-good flavour—a theory of justice for the common people. Yet it is this common sense that most needs unpacking.[4] The common sense surrounding restorative justice produces knowledge and ideas about criminal offending, about victimisation, and about the role of institutions and community. Broader social relations, particularly of class, race and gender, apparently disappear. In this context the common sense of restorative justice may sustain dominant social relations: the class and racialised underpinnings of the criminal justice system, the gendered nature of much interpersonal violence and the role of state violence may be left untouched through the commonsense logic of a restorative process. Rather

---

[3] Nils Christie, 'Conflicts as Property' (1977) 17 *British Journal of Criminology* 1.

[4] I am drawing on Gramsci's idea of 'common sense' as partial and incomplete. It may explain some aspects of the social world but is unable to explain broader patterns of social, economic and political power. Indeed common sense serves to embed specific cultural norms and ideologies as natural or inevitable features of the social world.

than providing a critical challenge to the status quo, restorative justice may simply serve an ideological function of reinforcing the dominant view of crime as individual pathology.

Common sense can be seen as contradictory and disparate. The ideas and knowledge which are found in social practices are not necessarily coherent. There is some merit in conceptualising restorative justice in this way, particularly given that the story of restorative justice is one of optimism, reform and social change. Yet restorative justice also demonstrates a strong tendency to work within traditional criminal justice systems and, whilst doing so, fails to challenge the exclusionary processes of criminalisation. Indeed, both a theory and a politics of criminalisation seems to be absent from the restorative justice literature. The role of the police and the law more generally in defining and constructing individuals and social groups as 'offenders' is left unexamined. The role of law in transmitting particular sets of ideas, attitudes and values, and how this might apply to the positioning of restorative justice within a broader legal system have been left largely unexplored. Nor is there adequate attention to the interrelationship between state power, law and the role that restorative justice might play in the broader struggle to maintain hegemony. The coercive aspects of state power which ultimately support the criminal justice system cannot be seen simply in contradistinction to the promise of restorative justice. As I argue later in this essay, the coercive functions of state power, and the legitimation functions of the law (particularly criminal law), ultimately underlie whatever role restorative justice might find within or beside criminal justice systems.

Despite the tendency to see restorative justice as outside the criminal justice system, it is by and large a regulatory mode of intervention with its particular subjects of regulation (the offenders and victims who participate in a conference for example) and agents of regulation (the state-employed conference convenors, often the police and sometimes the courts in an overseer role). It has its own strategies and processes (the legislative and administrative frameworks within which restorative justice occurs), sanctions (the criminal law for those offenders who fail) and the broader production of regulatory knowledge (the restorative justice evaluative literature for example).[5] Regulation also creates its own range of resistances and avoidances—it is a productive process with multiple outcomes. We can see some of those resistances in the refusal by some victims and offenders to participate in restorative processes—often defined as *failure* by those who control and evaluate.

A key argument in this essay is that restorative justice can be seen as a discourse which is consonant with neo-liberalism to the extent that it focuses on the 'active' responsibility of individual subjects: the responsibility of the offender for the particular crime, and the responsibility of the victim to participate in a process to restore his or her losses. Further, the process itself ostensibly rejects a key role for the state and privileges ownership by the community, while at the same time facilitating further state penetration of the community through the regulatory framework within which restorative justice operates.[6] A related argument in this regard is that restorative justice practices have emerged in increasingly bifurcated criminal justice systems, which regulate access to restorative justice programs on the basis of recidivism and risk. To the extent that Garland's concepts of criminologies of the 'self' and 'other' apply in this context, it is the 'self' (offenders who are rational actors like 'us') who receive the benefits of restorative justice; the 'other' (offenders who are racialised, marginalised and demonised) are sent packing for very long periods of time behind bars.[7] As I argue further in this essay, restorative justice can be understood only within the broader framework of criminal justice policies which have emphasised mass imprisonment and incapacitation.

The critique of restorative justice presented in this essay is not completely unsympathetic. It is a discussion of restorative justice within the context of unfulfilled possibilities. It still implies a

---

[5] For a discussion of regulatory modes of intervention, see A Hunt, *Explorations in Law and Society* (New York, Routledge, 1993) 315–20.

[6] P O'Malley, 'Risk and Restorative Justice: Governing Through the Democratic Minimisation of Harms' in I Aertsen, T Daems and L Robert (eds), *Institutionalizing Restorative Justice* (Devon, Willan Publishing, 2006) 221–22.

[7] D Garland, *The Culture of Control: Crime and Social Order in Contemporary Society* (Oxford, Oxford University Press, 2001).

contemplation of the restorative justice that might be. Certainly, the restorative justice movement sees itself as a radical social movement; yet it is often not deeply reflexive about the nature of power and its own position within contemporary criminal justice systems.[8] I do not believe there is anything inherent to restorative justice that prevents it from being used alongside repressive crime control strategies. Indeed there are already many examples of such a coalition of criminal justice strategies in place. However, what attracts me to restorative justice is a potential for social change in the way we do justice and a promise of alternative practice. This essay concentrates on the failings of restorative justice. But underpinning this discussion is a view of the possibilities for a more critical and reflexive restorative justice praxis—that is, a more developed and mutually responsive *theory* and *practice* which might bring about more sustained change.

The arguments I present in this essay derive from a range of different perspectives. These theoretical positions can broadly be grouped as neo-marxist, postmodernist, feminist and postcolonial. I am not suggesting that these perspectives provide internally consistent positions on restorative justice. Not surprisingly, there are often intersections, overlaps and contradictions. These critiques cover various points relating to the role of the state and its agencies, concepts of victim and offender and of globalisation and community, relations of class, 'race', ethnicity and gender, and questions about the rule of law, legal principles and appropriate process. What they have in common is a demand that we ask the questions: What role does restorative justice play in the reproduction of inequalities of class, race and gender? What are relations of power and resistance, and how does restorative justice articulate with other modes of punishment within neo-liberal regimes? These analytical frameworks provide us with the opportunity to pull apart the 'common sense' claims made by restorative justice

---

[8]   I am using the concept of reflexivity, as it is understood in social science, to refer to the act of self-reference where one critically examines one's own position within the social structure and how one's ideas and values both shape and are shaped by broader structures of power.

advocates, and to understand the elements of the appeal of restorative justice. They demand we go beyond the claims of restorative justice to truth, universalism and healing.

II. WHY RESTORATIVE JUSTICE

There is an abiding set of questions relating to the development of restorative justice over the last 20 to 30 years. Why does restorative justice emerge in a number of Western jurisdictions at a particular moment around the late 1980s and early 1990s, and then continue to proliferate over the next two decades? And why does it emerge with a relatively high degree of acceptance in many jurisdictions? How is it that within the space of a decade restorative justice finds its way onto the United Nations agenda—the Economic and Social Council adopted the *Basic Principles on the Use of Restorative Justice Programs in Criminal Matters* in 2002—and appears to be the answer not only to domestic crime problems, but also to international crimes and human rights abuses in transitional societies?

How is it that restorative justice emerges as a commonsense reform acceptable to a broad variety of political views and in differing national jurisdictions? The following section of this essay sets out to answer this question through the consideration of the universal pretensions of restorative justice—its concept of origins—and its appeal to those longing for greater communitarian approaches to justice. Lastly, restorative justice's place in the globalised transfer of criminal justice theory and practice is considered.

A. Concept of Origins

The 'advocacy' literature on the origins of restorative justice, much of which seems to obfuscate more than clarify the emergence of restorative justice, does little to explain credibly why or how restorative justice appears at a particular historical juncture and increasingly within a globalised context. The contemporary roots of restorative justice are said to be found in a range of different approaches in criminology and law emerging during the 1960s and 1970s that provide a broader milieu for the contemporary development of restorative justice as akin to a 'social movement'. These origins include the development of 'informal' justice, including victim–offender mediation, and in particular the rise of the victims' movement. In addition, a number of intellectual traditions supported the development of restorative justice, including European critical traditions of abolitionism, religious traditions stressing reconciliation and healing, and in North America, Australia and New Zealand those who stressed the values of indigenous cultures and dispute resolution processes in pre-state societies.[9]

The search for origins of restorative justice in indigenous traditions provided an important rhetorical tool to distinguish restorative justice traditions from modern state-centred systems of punishment. Some of the early examples of restorative justice were said to be found in family group conferencing in New Zealand in the late 1980s. Conferencing processes were said, at the time, to be linked to Maori dispute resolution processes. In relation to the development of punishment in the West, it was argued that the processes for ensuring that offenders made up for wrongdoings through restitution to the victim were eroded as the state assumed a central role in prosecuting and punishing offenders. The role of the community in owning the processes of dispute resolution was lost. Restorative justice was presented as alternative to state-centred justice and as a way of returning the resolution of 'conflicts' to the community. Thus the broad argument put by restorative justice advocates is that over the longer period of human history, the state assumed the function of punishment only relatively recently and that, previously, societies functioned well with restorative forms of sanctioning. Restorative methods of dispute resolution were dominant in non-state, pre-state and early state societies: individuals were bound closely to the social group, and mediation and restitution were primary ways of dealing with conflict. Further,

---

[9] K Daly and R Immarigeon, 'The Past, Present and Future of Restorative Justice: Some Critical Reflections' (1998) 1 *Contemporary Justice Review* 21; G Pavlich, *Governing Paradoxes of Restorative Justice* (London, Glasshouse Press, 2005).

these pre-modern, pre-state restorative forms of sanctioning can still be found being practised in indigenous communities today.

There are a number of assumptions underpinning this story of restorative justice. Most important for the current discussion are the simple dichotomies: non-state sanctioning is restorative (and, conversely, state-imposed punishment is not), and indigenous societies and pre-modern societies do not use utilise retributive forms of punishment as their primary mode of dispute resolution. Adding to the difficulties of separating fact from fiction have been some grandiose claims made by advocates. For example, John Braithwaite claimed that restorative justice was grounded in traditions of justice from the ancient Arab, Greek and Roman civilisations through to the public assemblies of the Germanic peoples, Indian Hindu, ancient Buddhist, Taoist and Confucian traditions. He concluded that 'restorative justice has been the dominant model of criminal justice throughout most of human history for all the world's peoples'.[10] It is difficult to think of a more far-reaching claim for legitimacy. As Daly has noted, these extraordinary claims need to be seen in a particular setting.[11] They are not 'authoritative histories' of justice, but attempts to construct origin myths about restorative justice. If it can be established that the first form of human justice was restorative then advocates can claim legitimacy for contemporary restorative justice alternatives to state-sponsored retributive justice. It may be argued that the use of history in this way is selective and fanciful. It both distorts the past and seeks to influence current choices. I would add that not only do these claims about the origins of restorative justice seek to establish a traditional legitimacy based on historical continuity, the claims also importantly attempt to establish the universalism of restorative justice 'for all the world's peoples'.

An example of this problem of selectivity has been the linking of restorative justice with restitution and the argument that restitution

---

[10] J Braithwaite, 'Restorative Justice: Assessing Optimistic and Pessimistic Accounts' in M Tonry (ed), *Crime and Justice: A Review of Research* (Chicago, University of Chicago Press, 1999) 25.

[11] Daly, above n 2, at 62.

was the dominant response in pre-state (or 'acephalous') societies. According to this argument, in pre-state societies blood feuds were replaced by restitution, and this became predominantly used as a system of crime control. Furthermore, restitution is seen as inherently victim-orientated and aimed at restoring balance. As Sylvester notes, 'these conclusions are aggressive statements of historical legitimacy that ... are often unsupported by the evidence'.[12] Simply seeing restitution as a more enlightened approach to justice can overlook that restitutive penalties were hierarchically based on class, clan and gender, and that serious consequences (including death) ensued where offenders were unable to meet restitution demands. It has been argued that historically, restitution was only marginally centred on victims and not all victims were equal.[13] The respective status of offender, victim and the community were all of central concern in determining penalty.[14]

Another aspect of the myths of origin relates to the often-made claim that restorative justice arose out of the growing contemporary concern with victims' needs and the development of the victims' rights movement. Again this is perhaps at best a partial truth. Certainly restorative justice can be seen in the context of the 'victimological turn' since the 1960s. Bottoms suggests that restorative justice may be useful to policy makers because it provides elements of moral clarification and moral pedagogy in its response to victims and their harms, and this also partially explains why restorative justice has been concentrated in areas of juvenile justice, because young people are seen as the most likely to benefit from moral pedagogy.[15]

However, as Richards has shown, the relationship between restorative justice and victim's rights is far more complex and nuanced than implied by the claim that restorative justice arose of a

---

[12] D J Sylvester, 'Myth in Restorative Justice History' (2003) 1 *Utah Law Review* 471 at 483.

[13] *Ibid* at 503.

[14] *Ibid.*

[15] A Bottoms, 'Some Sociological Reflections on Restorative Justice' in A Hirsch, J Roberts and A Bottoms, *Restorative Justice and Criminal Justice: Competing or Reconcilable Paradigms* (Oxford, Hart Publishing, 2003).

concern with victims.[16] At the very least, the development of the victims' movement grew out of a concern with serious offences like homicide, child abuse and rape, while restorative justice originally tended to be concerned with juveniles and more minor offending. Similarly, victims' desire to be heard in the justice system arose primarily from their experiences of serious criminal offences. Lastly, the claim to victim-friendly status seems to derive as much from a view that victims can rehabilitate offenders through the restorative justice process as from an intrinsic connection between restorative justice and victims' desires or needs.[17] Understanding the development of the victims' movement itself is problematic. Rock has argued that victims were largely an unknowable and incoherent group until the development of crime victimisation surveys.[18] The gathering of data on victims of crime constituted the group for whom policy was then developed. In this context restorative justice has found itself a place in policy responses to victims, particularly in juvenile justice matters.

Early restorative justice advocates in Australia, New Zealand and Canada developed their approaches by drawing on connections to indigenous cultures. As noted previously, family group conferencing in Australia and New Zealand was said to have been inspired by indigenous traditions. 'Sentencing circles' began in Canada in the 1990s in response to indigenous demands for more effective sentencing, while American 'peace-making' criminology also drew inspiration from native American traditions.

The search for restorative justice in indigenous traditions of dispute resolution has also led to claims which grossly over-simplify indigenous cultures. As Daly notes, the

> reverence for and romanticisation of an Indigenous past slide over practices that the modern 'civilised' Western mind would object to, such as a variety of harsh physical (bodily) punishments and banishment.[19]

[16] K Richards, 'Taking Victims Seriously? The Role of Victim's Rights Movements in the Emergence of Restorative Justice' (2009) 21 *Current Issues in Criminal Justice* 302.

[17] G Johnstone, *Restorative Justice: Ideas, Values, Debates* (Devon, Willan Publishing, 2002) 81.

[18] P Rock, *Helping Victims of Crime* (Oxford, Clarendon Press, 1990).

[19] Daly, above n 2, at 62.

There was also a much broader political context to the linking of restorative justice and indigenous justice. Part of the interest in indigenous forms of justice derived from the renewed political assertion of rights by indigenous groups in the former British 'settler' colonies of North America, Australia and New Zealand from the 1970s onwards.

Indigenous demands for recognition of customary law and land rights brought attention to indigenous modes of social control, and indigenous leaders themselves would sometimes articulate their claims for the legitimacy of indigenous law within the language of restorative justice. It was perhaps not difficult in this context to assume a homogeneous linking of interests between indigenous cultures and restorative justice.[20]

The Navajo Nation in the USA provides an example of the link between restorative justice and the rejuvenation of indigenous law. A revival of Navajo justice principles and processes began in the 1980s. The Navajo customs, usages and traditions came to form what has been called the Navajo common law.[21] The Navajo system is based on peace-making, described as a healing process aimed at restoring good relationships among people. Navajo methods seek to educate offenders about the nature of their behaviours and how they impact on others, and to help people identify their place in the community and reintegrate into community roles. 'Peace-making is based on relationships. It uses the deep emotions of respect, solidarity, self examination, problem-solving and ties to the community'.[22] Part of problem is the way restorative justice commentators have taken these processes, simplified their meaning and context, and universalised the process.

---

[20] E Zellerer and C Cunneen, 'Restorative Justice, Indigenous Justice and Human Rights' in G Bazemore and M Schiff (eds), *Restorative Community Justice: Repairing Harm and Transforming Communities* (Cincinnati, Anderson Press, 2001).

[21] R Yazzie and J Zion, 'Navajo Restorative Justice: The Law of Equality and Justice' in B Galaway and J Hudson (eds), *Restorative Justice: International Perspectives* (Monsey, Criminal Justice Press, 1996) 159.

[22] *Ibid*, at 170.

There is an implication that Navajo peacemaking represents a natural, authentic form of justice, a form abandoned by modern western societies in favour of a more 'artificial' system of state punitive justice.[23]

However, indigenous processes for maintaining social order and resolving disputes are diverse and complex. The United Nations estimates there are 300 million indigenous peoples globally, living in 70 nations spread over all continents. One might think that this basic fact should caution against claims of universalism made about indigenous restorative justice practices. The Yolngu people of Arnhemland in Australia and the Inuit of the Arctic Circle may have had some similar historical experiences of colonisation and subsequent social and political marginalisation, but their traditional social processes of resolving disputes are not necessarily 'restorative' simply because they are indigenous peoples. Given the diversity of indigenous cultures, it is not surprising that a variety of sanctions are used by indigenous peoples within their specific cultural frameworks. Certainly in most cases these sanctions are by definition 'non-state'.[24] However, are they restorative? Not surprisingly, some sanctions are 'restorative', in the sense that a modern proponent of restorative justice would accept, and some, clearly, are not. Indigenous sanctions might include temporary or permanent exile, withdrawal and separation within the community, public shaming of the individual, and restitution by the offender and/or his kin. Some sanctions may involve physical punishment such as beating or spearing. Discussions of Inuit and native American traditional punishments include the infliction of bodily punishments and, in severe cases, death penalties.[25] More generally these systems of punishment (like state-centred punishment) relied on the threat of force.

---

[23] Johnstone, above n 17, at 44.

[24] The exception might be in post-colonial societies where the dominant indigenous group ensures state control through exclusion of other minorities (eg, Fiji). But even here it is likely that international pressure will ensure that the state legal system at least resembles one that is friendly to the interests of the West: see M Findlay, *The Globalisation of Crime: understanding transitional relationships in context* (Cambridge, Cambridge University Press, 1999).

[25] Sylvester, above n 12, at 502–05.

There are a number of lessons to draw from this. First, indigenous societies deploy a range of sanctions depending on the seriousness of the offending behaviour. The definition of 'seriousness' will arise within specific cultural frameworks, as will the modes of punishment. We could legitimately characterise indigenous sanctions as covering traditional sentencing goals of retribution, deterrence, public denunciation, restitution and reparation. Certainly, restitution to the victim is an important goal, but it would be incorrect to see it as the only the goal. Physical punishments seem to display a strong element of retribution. Secondly, many of the sanctions are based on avoidance rather than confrontation between offender and victim. Temporary or permanent exile of the offender, or enforced avoidance between the offender and the victim, may certainly restore harmony to the community, but it is not a process which would normally find favour with restorative justice advocates. It is certainly not a process that is based on a principle of reintegration.

Restorative justice has had a tendency to romanticise indigenous dispute resolution. Blagg has argued that this romanticisation is a type of *Orientalism*—a concept referring to the way the West develops a complex set of representations for constructing and understanding the 'Other'.[26] In this case restorative justice discourses have come to construct indigenous justice mechanisms which are devoid of political, cultural and historical contexts:

> Through the Orientalist lens, distinctive and historically embedded cultural practices are essentialised, reduced to a series of discrete elements, then reassembled and repackaged to meet the requirements of the dominant culture.[27]

Certainly the early introduction of restorative justice processes in Canada, New Zealand and Australia supports Blagg's contention. New Zealand was the first jurisdiction to take up restorative justice

---

[26]   H Blagg, 'A Just Measure of Shame' (1997) 37 *British Journal of Criminology* 481; H Blagg, 'Aboriginal Youth and Restorative Justice: Critical Notes from the Frontier' in A Morris and G Maxwell (eds), *Restorative Justice for Juveniles* (Oxford, Hart Publishing, 2001).

[27]   Blagg, 'Aboriginal Youth and Restorative Justice', above n 26, at 230.

in a significant way, not as an indigenous practice but as a White, bureaucratic practice that was 'flexible and accommodating towards cultural difference' (that is, Maori culture).[28] However, it was often presented as an indigenous practice rather than, more mildly, as being *consistent* with indigenous practices. When restorative justice was introduced in New South Wales by police, it was largely claimed to be derived from indigenous practices. In Canada, sentencing circles were introduced by the courts to provide a more culturally appropriate form of sentencing for Aboriginal people in Canada. The point is that restorative justice processes were introduced and defined by non-indigenous criminal justice personnel claiming legitimation for these processes in traditional indigenous justice mechanisms. Ironically, the reconstruction and appropriation of idealised indigenous modes of social control and governance by restorative justice advocates may serve further to undermine indigenous political claims for self-determination because of the expectation that indigenous systems of control will be of a certain 'restorative' type.

At one level it is not difficult to point to the errors and assumptions made in the restorative justice literature on its 'origins', and this shortcoming has been consistently pointed out in the literature for more than a decade. The argument I am putting here is that it is more important that we understand the function of these truth claims in establishing the legitimacy and appeal of restorative justice. The importance of tying restorative justice to a vision of justice which is pre-state and indigenous is that it underscores two claims: restorative justice pre-dates state forms of punishment (thereby reinforcing the dichotomy of state versus community), and restorative justice has a universal claim to authenticity (restorative justice is beyond the context of time and place). These claims of authenticity and universalism support the commonsense appeal of restorative justice. The truth claim underpinning this commonsense appeal is that restorative justice is *naturally* superior to legal-bureaucratic forms of justice and it is a universal process available to all people.

---

[28] Daly, above n 2, at 62.

B. Explaining the Rise of Restorative Justice

The mythical origins of restorative justice attempt to establish its natural superiority to western legal forms of justice. However, we also need to identify and explain the political and historical contingencies that allowed for the undisputed growth in restorative justice during the 1990s and early 2000s. What were the conditions of possibility, the specific historical dynamics that allowed restorative justice to sustain itself and spread across various jurisdictions? There are essentially two interrelated questions here: Why has restorative justice emerged now? And why has it succeeded as a policy transfer across domestic and international jurisdictions? In answering these questions we can also begin to understand both the appeal and the limitations of restorative justice.

There are at least three broad responses to the 'Why now?' question. The self-serving answer of the restorative justice advocacy literature tends to rely on the points made previously: restorative justice has a universal appeal only temporarily abrogated by the ascendancy of state control of resolving disputes and responding to harms. A more developed explanation is to attribute the rise of restorative justice to a range of changes and developments which were occurring contemporaneously during the later part of the twentieth century. These include the rise of social movements in the 1960s and 1970s (such as feminist campaigns against male violence, and the absence of effective criminal justice responses; civil rights demands; indigenous political demands for greater self-determination and protests against segregation, deaths in custody and over-representation in the criminal justice system, and so on); the demand for reform of the criminal justice system by groups representing both prisoners' and victims' support and advocacy groups; the development of locally-based mediation and conflict resolution processes to deal with neighbourhood disputes; and the growing scepticism of public institutions and decline of trust in professionals.[29] In addition, a number of

[29] R Young and C Hoyle, 'Restorative Justice and Punishment' in W McConville (ed), *The Use of Punishment* (Devon, Willan Publishing, 2003).

other approaches supported the development of restorative justice, including 'informal' justice and abolitionism. While this contextual framework is no doubt important, the problem with the deployment of these various lists, which many restorative justice commentators use, is that it provides not so much an explanation as a group of associations. It does not explain why the state provides support for restorative justice, nor its popularity among those wishing to reform the criminal justice system.

Put briefly, other broad responses to the 'Why now?' question are, first, that restorative justice reflects a yearning for greater community involvement (*gemeinschaft*) in responses to crime that take an unambiguously moral position on crime; and, secondly, that restorative justice is consonant with a range of criminal justice discourses and broader political paradigms to be found in neo-liberalism. I suggest that these are not necessarily at odds with each other. The search for community and for definitive moral responses to crime can be seen in the context of neo-liberal demands for greater individual responsibility and accountability.

Bottoms has probably best put the *gemeinschaft* argument. Restorative justice is now an international movement, with some impact upon criminal justice systems, and appears to have come from a position of 'almost complete marginality' in the last 25 years. Yet, he suggests, it has remained small-scale and communitarian, without any consideration of current trends in penality such as risk assessment, managerialism, rising prison populations and so forth. Bottoms sees it as somewhat anomalous in contemporary penality, having grown 'within a penal policy context that in many ways seems to operate on a set of assumptions very different from its own'.[30] At least one answer to the question of why restorative justice has developed in this 'inauspicious' context is the appeal of the *gemeinschaft* in late modern societies.

According to Bottoms' argument, there are three different types of law, all of which may co-exist in any given jurisdiction: *gemeinschaft*, which is primarily concerned with the organic community;

---

[30] Bottoms, above n 15, at 100.

gesellschaft, which is concerned with the free, self-determining individual; and bureaucratic-administrative law, which has a focus on neither the organic human community nor the individual but on ruling interests, public policy and ongoing activities. The *gesellschaft*-type law may predominate as 'the foundation-stone of legal rules in any modern liberal-democratic state'.[31] There has also been a tendency in modern states to favour bureaucratic-administrative law, particularly in criminal law with the developments of risk management and managerialism. In this context there is perhaps a 'hunger' for *gemeinschaft*-type justice approaches which focus on community and civil society, and which could help to provide a counter-balance (or the appearance of a counter-balance) to *gesellschaft* and bureaucratic-administrative approaches to law and justice. While this search for *gemeinschaft* could be purely nostalgic, it could also be a genuine search for 'an organic rather than a bureaucratic approach to at least some supra-individual requirements within modern legal systems'.[32] Certainly the restorative justice literature prioritises the role of communities in supporting victims and reintegratively shaming offenders for their wrongful acts.

The search for *gemeinschaft* might explain why restorative justice has appeared in contemporary western legal systems whose main orientation is individualised justice within risk and managerialist frameworks. Following on from this, Bottoms makes two important points. First, restorative justice practices are 'only allowed to exist in certain spaces of late modern societies where it is thought that a *gemeinschaft* approach might have some value'.[33] Secondly, the structural space where restorative justice has been most developed, where it has been defined and positioned as most appropriate, is the area of youth justice.

Greater community connection to law also can be usefully connected to the role of restorative justice as an essentially moral approach to crime. *Gemeinschaft* and law's organic connection to community implies a clearly defined moral order. Undoubtedly,

---

[31] *Ibid*, at 101.
[32] *Ibid*, at 102.
[33] *Ibid*.

restorative justice views the engagement with offenders in a normative or moralising dialogue as a more effective way of responding to wrongdoing than punishment. Restorative justice is able to position itself as an approach separate from either retributive or rehabilitative approaches, and as one that unambiguously attempts to understand and respond to crime as a moral matter.

Although moral premises are part and parcel of every response to crime, it [the moral perspective] is characteristic of restorative justice, because the moral—or ethical—perspective is dominant in the very idea of restoration. Restorative justice defines, more or less explicitly, crime as a moral act for which the offender—as a moral subject—is responsible and accountable . . . [T]he offender is addressed as a moral subject who has harmed another person.[34]

In this regard restorative justice constructs individuals as moral subjects with common moral understandings, and imposes on them certain expectations about appropriate behaviour—an understanding seen as particularly appropriate to juveniles, but also one that can be expanded to certain adult offenders (those who are not demonised), to victims (who are presented with an essentially moral obligation to meet with the offender and forgive), and indeed to collective actions and historical harms (through truth and reconciliation processes). The strongly moralistic flavour of restorative justice sits well with both communitarian approaches, which stress the role of community in reintegrating the wrong-doing offender and the wronged victim, and the views of those conservatives who wish to emphasise individual responsibility and moral culpability.

Thus we can bring together the *gemeinschaft* and moral appeals of restorative justice in understanding its growing acceptance. The yearning for *gemeinschaft* clarifies the communitarian appeal of restorative justice, while the unambiguous delineation of right and wrong and the moral demands placed on the offender are appealing

[34] H Boutellier, 'Victimalization and restorative justice: moral backgrounds and political consequences' in L Walgrave (ed), *Restorative Justice and the Law* (Devon, Willan Publishing, 2002) 21.

to a justice system increasingly dominated by the segregation and management of individuals and groups on the basis of risk and public protection, by a system and process that is often amoral in its application. Recasting these two arguments slightly, we can understand the appeal of restorative justice as a means of providing *social connectedness* and *moral certainty*. Restorative justice challenges neither justice based on individual responsibility and accountability, nor the management of offenders, crime and the potentiality for crime (pre-crime) on the basis of risk analysis. It is essentially an addition to these existing modes of understanding and operationalising justice. If we return to the notion of common sense, we can argue that the *gemeinschaft* (or social connectedness) and moral certainty apparently provided by restorative justice play an important function in securing consent to a justice system which is largely devoid of either of these two features, and which in its vast majority of responses to crime is not restorative at all. Restorative justice remains on the periphery, exciting the intellects of academics and some practitioners, while the criminal justice system continues largely with business as usual, processing individuals through routine institutional practices and a set repertoire of responses. Rather than challenging the established institutional response, restorative justice provides a diversion—a *divertissement*—which apparently shows that justice is connected to the community and is about commonsense notions of clearly delineated right and wrong. Meanwhile, that quintessentially amoral measure of all value, the monetary fine, is 'the most frequently used means of punishing, deterring, compensating and regulating throughout the legal system'.[35]

A common argument put by advocates is that restorative justice has emerged as a response to the failure of existing criminal justice systems. As Richards has noted in her review of these arguments, 'the notion of a failed criminal justice system has been cited historically in order to justify and explain a whole range of new crime

---

[35] P O'Malley, *The Currency of Justice: Fines and Damages in Consumer Societies* (Abingdon, Routledge-Cavendish, 2009) 1.

control initiatives'.[36] What is important to explain is how restorative justice becomes a possibility at a particular historical juncture. The final argument I want to consider in relation to the rise of restorative justice is its connection to the developments of neoliberalism. Changes in the late modern state have seen a decline of welfarism and the rise of neo-liberal governance, with less focus on the social context of crime and more emphasis on the individual, the family and the community in terms of responsibility and accountability.[37] This change has been referred to as a preference for 'governing at a distance', where government seeks to act more through local associations. Further, the 'death of the social' has seen both new forms of governance and a move away from social benefits and social welfare which are said to create dependency. In the place of universal entitlement to social welfare is 'mutual obligation': a demand for autonomous individuals who are not dependent on the state, and that any state assistance should come with a range of enforceable obligations attached.

The emphasis on individual and community responsibility and accountability has been referred to as 'responsibilisation'. According to Garland, the process of responsibilisation relates to the partial transference of state crime control to community-based and non-state individuals and organisations.[38] Government still seeks to act upon crime but does so more indirectly through local bodies, community organisations and individuals. Through 'governing at a distance', responsibility is pushed down into local authorities (such as schools) and partnerships between criminal justice agencies and the public (for example, neighbourhood watch). One aspect of responsibilisation is placing requirements on individuals to be engaged in self-help and to be active citizens. It is

---

[36] K Richards, 'Cause and Effect? Failings of the Contemporary Penal System and the Emergence of Restorative Justice' in J Gaffey, A Possamai-Inesedy and K Richards (eds), *The Chameleon and the Quilt* (Penrith, University of Western Sydney, 2005) 48.

[37] See Garland, above n 7.

[38] D Garland, 'The Limits of the Sovereign State' (1996) 36 *British Journal of Criminology*. 445.

not about the state off-loading its functions; rather, it is a new mode of exercising power and of governing crime, with its own forms of knowledge, objectives, techniques and apparatuses.

> The state does not diminish or become merely a nightwatchman. On the contrary it retains all its traditional functions—the state agencies have actually increased their size and output during the same period—and, in addition, takes on a new set of co-ordinating and activating roles . . .[39]

The realignment of values and approaches within justice systems which occurred from the late 1970s onwards, particularly in juvenile justice, emphasised deeds over needs. The focus shifted from a welfare-aligned rehabilitative approach to a justice-orientated approach with an emphasis on deterrence and retribution. Individual responsibility and accountability increasingly became the focus of the way justice systems approached offenders. In this context seemingly contradictory processes are at play which include, for example, restorative justice and incapacitation, and which combine neo-conservative approaches with neo-liberalism).[40] The privatisation of institutions and services, widening social and economic inequality, and new or renewed insecurities around fear of crime, terrorism, 'illegal' immigrants and racial, religious and ethnic minorities all impact on the way criminal justice systems operate. All of which has fuelled demands for centralised authoritarian law and order strategies, a focus on pre-crime and actual crime, and a push for 'what works' responses to crime and disorder.[41]

More specifically, state support for restorative justice can be seen in the context of responsibilisation. It allows for 'government at a distance' through apparent community involvement in securing individual responsibility for criminal offending, and does so in

[39] *Ibid*, at 454.

[40] P O'Malley, 'Volatile and Contradictory Punishments' (1999) 3 *Theoretical Criminology* 175.

[41] J Muncie, 'The globalization of crime control—the case of youth and juvenile justice: Neo-liberalism, policy convergence and international conventions' (2005) 9 *Theoretical Criminology* 35 at 37.

a way which stresses social solidarity. Responsibilisation extends beyond the offender. In restorative justice matters involving young people, the parents are brought into a role of taking responsibility for their child's behaviour. The victim also becomes a 'responsibilised' partner in the crime control process. As in programs like neighbourhood watch, the victim is required to play an active role in reducing crime—in this case through assisting in the reformation of the offender. Further, the increasingly bifurcated approach does not result in the state relinquishing control of crime. Indeed, through more punitive approaches to policing and sentencing, serious offenders and repeat offenders are treated more harshly than ever.

We return to the question of bifurcation and more punitive law and order approaches later in this essay. For now it is sufficient to note why the state supports some aspects of restorative justice, and why it is primarily confined to less serious offending and less serious offenders at the 'lower reaches of the system'.[42] It seems to me that restorative justice is consonant with a general move in criminal justice systems in the late 1980s and 1990s which broadly can be explained within neo-liberal politics. Although presented by its advocates as a reforming alternative, restorative justice fits with broader processes of governance at a distance and responsibilising individuals and communities in the task of crime control. Rather than challenging state power it allows for new modes of governance. It appeals to those who long for greater communitarian approaches, while at the same time developing a strongly moralistic framework for dealing with offenders.

C. Policy Transfer and the Globalisation of Restorative Justice

Over the last decade there has been considerable discussion about how ideas of crime control and specific policies and practices move between states. At the broadest level shifts in economic and social

[42] Young and Hoyle, above n 29.

structures and changes in cultural sensibilities are seen as explaining potential convergences of crime control.[43] Globalisation suggests a growing international economic, political, legal and cultural interconnectedness through advances in technology, international law, and neo-liberal economics and politics. It is often assumed that within this context criminal justice policies are converging worldwide. The developments of restorative justice across jurisdictions can be seen as a broader convergence of criminal justice policy, at least in the Anglophone world and parts of Europe.

Jones and Newburn have discussed more specific dimensions of criminal justice policy convergence, particularly between the US and the UK, including convergence of policy content where there is a clear transfer of policy (for example prison privatisation). Other forms include convergence of policy style and symbolic politics, that is transfers of ideas and ideologies (such as zero-tolerance policing) rather than specific practices and policies. Lastly, there may be limited convergences where, although both the identified policy problems and the political rhetoric may be similar, the actual measures developed may be quite different (for example, the response to sex offenders). In the case of restorative justice there are examples of direct transfer of policy, such as the use of 'conferencing' practices for dealing with young offenders in the UK, Australia and New Zealand. However, the greatest transfer has been in the idea and ideology of restorative justice. Within this context there has been a proliferation of widely divergent restorative justice practices operating at various points in the criminal justice system across Europe and the Anglophone world. However, these all claim to adhere to a central framework of ideas which constitute restorative justice.

While there is a convergence in the ideas and rhetoric of restorative justice, there needs to be acknowledgement of the complexities and differences in restorative justice practice. Although the broad structural developments in neo-liberalism point to particular forms of crime control, and I have included restorative justice in

---

[43] Garland, above n 7.

these, the actual developments in specific jurisdictions are dependent on a range of factors. Karstedt has referred to the importance of path-dependency and diverse trajectories in the way crime policies are developed across jurisdictions.[44] As a result, crime policies are changed or developed in different ways as they travel across nations, affected by a range of historical, cultural, social and political factors. However, the recognition of different pathways does not imply that the process of policy transfer, or the policies themselves, cannot be linked to more structural explanations in the development of neo-liberalism.[45]

Muncie has discussed the growth of the 'what works' paradigm particularly in relation to juvenile justice, and the changes from the 'nothing works' pessimism of the late 1970s and early 1980s to a type of

> scientific realism that stresses rational planning, performance measurement, evidence-based research, and crime and disorder audits to identify programs to prevent crime and reduce re-offending.[46]

The ascendancy of the 'what works' paradigm has assisted the growth and transfer of restorative justice practices across jurisdictions. The positive evaluations of family group conferencing in New Zealand and then Australia in the late 1980s and early 1990s (including the involvement of Lawrence Sherman, a leading proponent of the 'what works' paradigm) enabled restorative justice to become firmly embedded within the 'what works' literature. In the UK, Walklate has suggested that New Labour, with its 'tough on crime and tough on the causes of crime' rhetoric, was keen to identify 'best practice' in juvenile justice and subsequently picked up the Thames Valley Police conferencing project (which had been based on the Australian and New Zealand models).[47]

---

[44] S Karstedt, 'Durkheim, Tarde and Beyond: The Global Travel of Crime Policies' in T Newburn and R Sparkes (eds), *Criminal Justice and Political Cultures. National and International Dimensions of Crime Control* (Devon, Willan Publishing, 2004).

[45] *Ibid*, at 23.

[46] J Muncie, 'Policy Transfers and "What Works": Some Reflections on Comparative Youth Justice' (2001) 1 *Youth Justice* 27 at 27.

[47] S Walklate, 'Researching Restorative Justice: Politics, Policy and Process' (2005) 13 *Critical Criminology* 165.

As policy makers became 'free to trawl the world for evidence of what seems to "work", to pilot "the promising" back home and to ensure that its success is "proven" through evaluation and continual re-evaluation', restorative justice increasingly became part of the new repertoire for youth justice interventions.[48] The irony here is that in many respects the policy transfer among Anglophone countries has tended to follow the more punitive lead of the USA, exemplified by zero-tolerance policing, boot camps, curfews, electronic monitoring, mandatory minimum sentences, shaming offenders and punishing parents. Furthermore, North American discourses on rehabilitation and risk management have been pervasive, particularly in relation to identifying risk factors and employing cognitive behavioural programs. Although restorative justice does not easily fit within the cognitive behavioural therapy programs that dominate the 'what works' suite of responses to offenders, it has been able, on the basis of numerous evaluations, to surmount the scientific threshold as a best practice model. Coupling the best-practice status with the communitarian and moral appeal of restorative justice outlined previously, we can begin to see why there has been momentum for its international transfer.

While there is a broad array of possible interventions, it is possible to see a framework of crime control strategies (which include restorative justice) which are held together broadly within a focus on risk, managerialism and responsibilisation. The transfer of restorative justice across international boundaries can at least partially been seen in this broader context of a growth of criminal justice policy movement, particularly between North America, Australasia and the UK. Restorative justice becomes essentially a peripheral component of an extensive list of possible interventions. It can be taken from the criminal justice menu as, perhaps, a more palatable element of a range of policies that are generally punitive and coercive.

---

[48] Muncie, above n 46, at 27.

However, we also need to guard against the idea that policy transfer is somehow an homogenised process across all states. There is less homogeneity of restorative justice practice in Europe, for example, and the implementation of restorative justice there is marked by greater diversity.

In Belgium, Finland and Norway, restoration is an extension of existing welfare, education or rehabilitative strategies. In England, as evidenced, for example, in its referral orders and youth offender panels, restoration is more authoritarian and paternalistic aimed at responsibilizing the offender. In Norway, victim–offender mediation is used as an *alternative* to judicial processing, whereas in most jurisdictions it is integrated into other criminal justice processes. Some systems are victim oriented (Denmark), some focus on the offender (France, Spain) and in others the orientation is mixed. Belgium employs restorative principles at all stages of the judicial process; in France and England and Wales it only operates at a pre- or trial stage, while in Denmark it is employed at the moment of sentence.[49]

There is clearly a heterogeneity of process and practice in restorative justice. Restorative justice becomes embedded within existing criminal justice and social policy frameworks. However, despite these various pathways, what is interesting is the proliferation of the *idea* of restorative justice across Europe—an idea which has emerged also at a time when, in general, European jurisdictions have seen a move towards greater use of risk-based strategies and growing reliance on the use of imprisonment as a crime control strategy.

An important part of the movement of restorative justice internationally and its claims to be a globalising force has been its acceptance onto the UN agenda. As Van Ness noted at the UN in 2005, 'in only 25 years, restorative justice has become a worldwide criminal justice reform dynamic. Well over 80 countries use some form of restorative practice in addressing crime'.[50] There is

---

[49] Muncie, above n 41, at 43.
[50] Cited in A Porter, 'Restorative justice takes the world stage at the United Nations Crime Congress', available at <www.realjustice.org/library/uncrimecongress.html>.

certainly no argument that restorative justice has spread and, indeed, been actively promoted at a global level. In 2002, the UN Economic and Social Council (ECOSOC) adopted the *Basic Principles on the Use of Restorative Justice Programs in Criminal Matters*. At the 11th UN Congress on Crime Prevention and Criminal Justice in 2005, restorative justice, along with 'enhancing criminal justice reform', was one of the six official congress workshops.

The adoption in 2002 of the *Basic Principles* was largely due to the Working Party on Restorative Justice. The Working Party was formed by the Alliance of Non-governmental Organizations (NGOs) on Crime Prevention and Criminal Justice, which is a US-based group. The majority of members of the Working Group were from the US, with a couple each from Australia and Europe, and one member from India. The composition of the Group does not detract from its achievement in having the *Basic Principles* adopted by the ECOSOC, but it does reflect the fact that the *internationalisation* of restorative justice is largely being driven by the US, with some assistance from Europe and Australia. The danger is that the globalised processes of restorative justice are being developed, defined and driven from within specific criminal justice contexts of a few first-world nations.

Globalisation has the effect of imparting preferred models of capitalist development, modernisation and urbanisation. In this context, globalisation increasingly demands particular forms of capital accumulation, as well as associated social and legal relations both within and between nation states. At first glance this may seem irrelevant to the localised claims of restorative justice. However, discussions around globalisation should alert us to the need to situate the growing interest in restorative justice within the shifting boundaries of relations within and between the first world and the third world. This is particularly the case when much restorative justice talk presents itself as an alternative narrative on justice, as something outside the justice paradigms of retribution, deterrence and rehabilitation, and as a form of resolving disputes which is 'non-Western'.

Little attention has been paid to whether restorative justice is as much as a part of a globalised justice as other, more traditional

Western legal forms. The potential of restorative justice to overwhelm local custom and law is as real as it is with other models built on retributivism or rehabilitation. The risk is that restricted and particularised notions of restorative justice will become part of a globalising tendency which restricts local justice mechanisms in areas where there is a demand to 'modernise'—and there have been examples of this in the Asia–Pacific region. Thus, actual localised customary and non-state practices for resolving disputes and harms will be replaced by what the West understands to be restorative justice—and we can see examples of this in Australia, where Aboriginal customary processes are seen as less legitimate than state-organised and sanctioned forms of restorative justice such as youth conferencing. Alternatively, traditional forms of localised justice may be forced to respond to crimes they were never designed to deal with in the interests of broader appeals to restorative justice—a point to which I return later in this essay in the discussion on the *gacaca* courts in Rwanda.

In summary, then, it is important to understand the appeal of restorative justice within the context of a particular common sense about the need for social connectedness and moral certainty. Restorative justice promises a new way of dealing with offenders and victims which seemingly allows for greater community involvement and an unambiguous process of determining right and wrong, moral blameworthiness, accountability and then forgiveness. Restorative justice establishes itself as the universal good, a process set for all time and all people beyond the relativity of culture and superior to the legal-bureaucratic state approaches of retribution. However, when we understand restorative justice within a particular context of late modern societies, we can see that it is a technique which fits well with the responsibilisation of individuals and the state governing at a distance through the community-based practices: the state is apparently removed from a direct role in punishment, and that role is returned to the community. Lastly, the international appeal of restorative justice lies in its acceptability to neo-liberal approaches to crime control. Restorative justice fits within paradigms of 'what works' and 'best practice', while at the same time it takes an unequivocally moral stance towards crime.

III. CREATING IDEAL VICTIMS AND OFFENDERS

Victims and offenders are at the core of restorative justice, and it places great expectations on these two groups to do certain things, to exhibit certain emotions and behave in certain ways. Certainly the ideal is that restorative justice will be beneficial for both victims and offenders. Victims will experience empowerment, healing and closure. They will be given the opportunity to ask questions about the offence and express their emotions. Offenders will confront the harm they have caused, take responsibility for their actions, apologise, act to repair the harm and as a result be accepted back into their community. One of the questions that puzzles me most about restorative justice is how people experience this process? By this I mean something more than whether the victim or the offender was 'satisfied' with the outcome of the process, or whether they thought the process was fair. I am also interested in the questions of subjectivity and identity which go to the heart of restorative justice. Does the 'ideal' victim or offender of restorative justice ever exist and, if not, what are the implications for the restorative process?

In restorative justice, as in most court processes, 'victim' and 'offender' are often understood as uncomplicated and homogeneous categories of self. There are no complexities here: a person is either an offender or a victim, and these universal categories appear to subsume all other possible identities. But can we assume that everyone subjectively experiences these categories in identical or, at least, similar ways, irrespective of their gender, class, race, ethnicity, sexual preference, religion or age? Victims and offenders are legal subjects who do not exist in a natural state separated from the social characteristics through which individuals live their lives. To be a citizen, to be a victim, to be a criminal takes on meaning only in the context of social relations between people and within the broader institutions of society. Perhaps, it could be argued, restorative justice allows us an opportunity to explore these social relations and their impact on crime and victimisation. However, given that most restorative justice processes are already firmly embedded within state practice, the identities of victim and offender and the script which is expected to be followed is already well established. There does not appear to be much opportunity to challenge these identities. Indeed, we must accept the label of ourselves as either an offender or as a victim before we are allowed to enter into established restorative justice processes. If we refuse, for example, to self-identify as an offender, we are precluded from engaging in the script of restorative justice.

Like the criminal law more generally, restorative justice narratives have tended to construct subjectivity as a binary field of either offender or victim, with little attention to the profound difficulties that underpin these classifications. In oppressed or marginalised communities many victims may also be offenders. The homeless teenager with drug and alcohol problems may be an offender one day and a victim of crime the next, although if she is homeless her own victimisation is unlikely to be reported or acted upon. And what of the cultural and racial differences we attribute to our understanding of victim and offender? Do we see and value a victim and an offender in the same way, irrespective of the cultural lens through which we construct and understand these categories? Given the profound racialisation of criminal justice systems, are minority victims and offenders seen in same light as members of the dominant group: are all offenders and victims of equal standing? What of the shaming process: can we be sure whether any shaming of the offender that takes place is either disintegrative or reintegrative? Is there enough social legitimacy in the process to support victims and to allow for reintegration of offenders?

The stereotypical concepts of victim and offender which appear in the restorative justice literature seem to me to be problematic. The ideal victim is the individual person who has been victimised by a (preferably unknown) offender engaging in a predatory crime such as a robbery, car theft or house burglary. It is less clear how we deal with different types of victims in the restorative justice process: for example, those that know their perpetrator or who are repeatedly victimised by those with whom they live. Similarly, restorative justice schemes which have been established do not seem to cover victims who live in institutions (such as young people in detention centres or adult prisoners). Those who are most marginalised as victims and offenders (such as those who are homeless, suffer mental illness or have intellectual disabilities, those with serious drug and alcohol problems—in other words, those who fill our courts and prisons on a daily basis) are least likely to engage in an articulate process designed to extract remorse and remedy an individual harm. The ability to articulate a particular narrative as an offender or a victim is fundamental to the restorative justice process.

A. The Victim

Restorative justice is often presented as according a high priority to victims: the process allows for victim participation and healing, and for a greater range of reparative outcomes than the traditional criminal justice system. However, not all victims want to be involved in either the criminal justice system or restorative justice programs. Existing research would seem to indicate that in the case of more minor offences there is a desire not to pursue the matter personally—witness, for example, the repeated findings in crime victim surveys which show a major reason for not reporting crime is the belief that it is too trivial or too unimportant. Surveys suggest that some victims may not want greater involvement: they may want only to be informed of developments, or not to be involved at all. Many are no longer interested in the case, or think that it is the responsibility of the police or other authorities to pursue; others are too busy, or want to forget the offence. Many do not want the responsibility of deciding an offender's future.[51]

---

[51] S Garkawe 'Restorative Justice from the Perspective of Crime Victims' (1999) 15 *Queensland University of Technology Law Journal* 40.

The 'victim' is not a homogeneous character singularly created out of his or her experience of crime. Even if they have an interest in the outcomes, not all victims will want to meet with the persons who committed offences against them. As Richards has suggested, there is probably an inverse relationship between the types of offences for which restorative justice practices are used (involving young offenders committing more minor offences) and the situations in which a victim may be likely to want to confront the offender (in relation to more serious offences).[52] For example, a common reason why victims decline to participate in victim–offender mediation is that they do not have the time or interest in participating. Do we perceive this as a lack of civic duty, or as a lack of social engagement? Is there something 'wrong' with the victim because he or she does not wish to participate in a pre-defined process largely foisted upon him or her? Or does it simply reflect that many individuals who suffer certain harms, such as having their car stolen, their property vandalised or their house robbed, prefer compensation to being actively engaged with reforming the offender?

If victims feel that they are being coerced to participate in a restorative justice conference (ironically, perhaps by people working *within* the criminal justice system or associated state agencies, such as police, court workers, social workers), the result may be secondary victimisation rather than victim empowerment. Indeed, where restorative justice practices are conducted with the threat of court or some other form of sanctioning in the background, the victim may not consider any apology on the part of the offender as real. Restorative 'coercion' may leave victims who participate in the process with a sense of cynicism. Existing research suggests that perhaps more than half of participating victims do not believe the offender's apology to be sincere.[53] At least one reason for this is that offenders are *not* sorry, while in other cases the victims may misread the communicative accounts provided by

---

[52] Richards, above n 16.
[53] K Daly, 'The Limits of Restorative Justice' in D Sullivan and L Tift (eds), *Handbook of Restorative Justice* (Abingdon, Routledge, 2006) 139–40.

the offender. Overall, though, we are left wondering about the validity of the claims that restorative justice provides cathartic release, victim empowerment, a consensual reparative outcome and reconciliation.

One of the criticisms of restorative justice is that in reality it is much more focused on the offender than the victim—it is about the reformation of the offender. The victim is to some extent peripheral to this process, except to the extent that his or her presence may assist in reforming the offender. As Wright has succinctly noted, victims may be promised healing, but the 'primary aims are crime reduction and re-education of the offender'.[54] Is it acceptable to use the victim to shame the offender? The participation of the victim may assist the offender to confront the offence and the harm which was caused, but is this an acceptable use of the victim? Can it amount 'to a form of "victim prostitution" in which victims are effectively "used" in order to bring about certain effects on offenders with a view to reducing the incidence of offending'?[55] Victim advocates have claimed with some justification that recognition of the offender has been at the centre of the design, implementation and development of restorative justice practices. This was evident, for example, in the low rate of victim participation in the Thames Valley conferencing scheme in the UK. Often victims were not available to attend at the set time, and the conference would proceed without them. Their presence was not essential, but the offender and 'professionals' were absolutely required.[56]

The low level of attendance of victims in youth justice conferencing has been noted previously in this essay. During the early years of operation in New Zealand, fewer than half the conferences had a victim present, and this was precisely at a time when the New Zealand family group conferencing model was being lauded

---

[54] M Wright, 'The Court as Last Resort: Victim-Sensitive, Community-Based Responses to Crime' (2002) 42 *British Journal of Criminology* 654 at 657.

[55] D Denham, N Olley and L Wolhuter, *Victimology: victimisation and victims' rights* (London, Routledge-Cavendish, 2008) 224.

[56] B Williams, *Victims of Crime and Community Justice* (London, Jessica Kingsley Publishers, 2005).

internationally as a successful example of restorative justice.[57] In South Australia it was found that local youth justice coordinators had insufficient resources to organise family group conferences. In working with Aboriginal young people, some of the most time-consuming and culturally difficult tasks involved the identification of family members who were appropriate to participate in the conference and then subsequently arranging for them to come together for a conference. It was noted that very few victims of offences were involved in the conferences, resulting in a central feature of the scheme being omitted from the process.[58]

Perhaps it is not surprising that many restorative justice processes have a poor victim participation rate. There are many reasons for the absence of victims in the larger conferencing programs, and these can relate to administrative and resourcing demands on the system as well as to victim choice not to participate. It is clear, however, that in practice much restorative justice occurs without a victim present. Restorative justice appears to place victims at the centre of its theoretical and normative framework, but in reality the processes occur regularly and apparently unproblematically without victim participation. In contrast, and despite the counter-positioning of restorative justice as an alternative to state sanctioning, few conferences proceed without representatives from various state agencies.

The lack of victim participation has important theoretical and practical implications. In theory a key distinction between criminal justice and restorative justice is that the criminal justice system names the offending behaviour as an offence against the state, while in restorative justice approaches the focus is on the victim and the harm suffered. Yet in reality, if the victim is absent, it is the convenor or facilitator of the restorative justice conference who essentially takes on the role of identifying and naming the harm,

---

[57] G Maxwell and A Morris, 'Research on Family Group Conferences with Young Offenders in New Zealand' in J Hudson *et al* (eds), *Family Group Conferences* (Leichardt, Federation Press, 1996).

[58] C Cunneen, 'Community Conferencing and the Fiction of Indigenous Control' (1997) 30 *Australia and New Zealand Journal of Criminology* 292.

and plays a key role in the search for reparation. The convenor acts within a legal and administrative framework established by the state. It is the state with the full force of law that 'calls' the conference. Law *interpellates* us and places us in our respective positions and roles as victims and offenders. It seems to be disingenuous to claim that this process somehow rebalances the focus of responding to harm away from the state and back to the community and the victim. At best it changes the players and dramaturgical script away from the court process, but it does not shift significantly the role of the state in defining and responding to criminal behaviour, neither does it change the script in naming us as victims (or offenders) and placing a certain expectation, or indeed obligation, to behave in certain ways (eg remorseful, apologetic, forgiving). Even this script is in some ways dissembling, because in the absence of the actual victim, a quasi-representative of the state and community (the convenor) becomes the victim-equivalent for the duration of the restorative process.

B. Victim Trauma

One of the most worrying aspects of restorative justice is the assumption it makes about a victim's ability to confront an offender and extend forgiveness. The accepted restorative justice wisdom is that victims will benefit from the opportunity to hear from the offender about the reasons why the offence was committed, to put a 'face' to the offender and to articulate the harm caused by the offence. However, the level of unresolved trauma and grief with which a victim of serious crime lives will be inverse to his or her willingness to engage in a restorative justice exercise with an offender. This can be the case with primary victims of, for example, sexual assault, and secondary victims, particularly family members of a child or partner who has been murdered.

The idea that a victim of serious crime can resolve his or her grief and loss through a meeting with the offender can be seriously misplaced. This is not to suggest he or she may be seeking punitive retribution against the offender—this may or may not be the case. Rather, what is at stake is whether the restorative justice process will in fact do more harm to the victim than if a traditional prosecution and court outcome were to take place. A person suffering unresolved grief, or indeed post-traumatic stress, is unlikely to be 'satisfied' with either restorative justice or a traditional court sentencing process. While there may be a desire by the victim to 'confront' the offender, the pressure to reach a reconciliation or a reparative outcome may be counterproductive.

As Daly has noted, victims experience crime differently, 'some are only lightly touched, whereas others experience many disabling effects such as health problems, sleeplessness, loss of self-confidence, among others'.[59] Victims who have high distress levels are not likely to be assisted by restorative justice processes. They are likely to need counselling and specific material assistance before they can be expected to 'dispense the spiritual balm and experience the psychological release that restorative theorists envision'.[60] The evidence from the evaluation of the South Australian juvenile restorative justice program suggests that while victims and offenders saw the process as fair, the victim's level of distress affected the outcome of the conference and his or her longer-term recovery. Those who were more distressed or suffered from greater levels of trauma were less able to engage in the restorative justice process. Thus the character and experience of victimisation is directly related to whether restorative justice outcomes are achieved for the victim. Those victimisation effects and the restorative justice experiences are mediated by the gender of the victim, the type of crime and a range of other factors.[61] This research suggests that greater levels of victimisation (in the sense of ongoing trauma) make restorative justice programs less appropriate for the victim.

---

[59] Daly, above n 53, at 140.
[60] E Waldman, 'Restorative Justice and the Pre-conditions for Grace: Taking Victim's Needs Seriously' (2007) 9 *Cardozo Journal of Conflict Resolution* 91 at 93.
[61] Daly, above n 53, at 141.

As Waldman notes, some victims may never be ready for restorative justice.[62] They may never reach a point where they can offer the forgiveness and empathy required of them. I was reminded of this at a conference on reconstruction and reparations held in Cape Town, South Africa in early 2001. The conference included a visit to the former apartheid-era prison on Robben Island. Tours of the prison, now a world heritage site, are undertaken by former political prisoners. Our guide told us he had spent five years there—according to him, a relatively short time compared to many other prisoners. In a matter-of-fact manner he told us that his former torturer had visited the island the previous year with his wife and children, and had apologised for his actions. Our guide responded that the apology was all very fine, but as a result of the torture he and his wife would never have children. I did not detect any bitterness, hatred or forgiveness when he told this story—just a chasm that separated him from the emotions that perhaps might be expected. But then I was left wondering why we should *expect* forgiveness from victims any more than we should expect a range of other possible responses.

Restorative justice is often presented as if it is beneficial to all victims alike, irrespective of their own understandings and experiences. The question of 'victimhood' is further compounded, however, when we consider that the status and identity of victims can vary substantially. How suitable are restorative justice initiatives for dealing with cases in which the 'identity' or 'status' of the victim is in some way problematic? Victims may be indirect or secondary victims. There are situations where the victim or the offender is not an individual person. These might be government bodies or private corporations, ranging from a small business to transnational corporations. One situation of particular interest in relation to offences committed by young people is where the victim is the arresting police officer. A significant proportion of offences committed by young people relate to public disorder. In many public order cases it is the police officer who exercises his or her discretion

---

[62] Waldman, above n 60.

to be offended by particular behaviour or language—there is no specific victim other than the police officer. Can we say with any degree of certainty that the police officer's 'victimhood' stands representative of the community more generally? One might question whether the officer's role as victim in a restorative process is appropriate when he or she is also responsible for detecting and prosecuting offenders.

C. Does Restorative Justice Offer a Better Deal for Victims?

There is a range of difficulties in assessing whether restorative justice responds well to the needs of victims. These arise not only from individual differences between victims and their experiences, but also from differing restorative justice practices, variations in the relationship between restorative justice and the criminal justice system (for example, 'How involved are police or prosecutors?', 'Are restorative justice outcomes enforceable by a court?' etc), and in the offence types and categories of offenders for which restorative justice is available (for example, 'Which offences are excluded from restorative justice?', 'Are repeat offenders or serious offenders excluded?').

While noting the significant differences which exist in the way restorative justice programs actually operate, it is worth considering in more detail whether our experiences with restorative justice indicate that it actually offers a better deal than a more traditional (adversarial) court setting. Herman usefully sets out a number of ways in which the requirements of legal proceedings are opposed to the interests of victims.[63] I follow each of these points with a note about whether restorative justice does things better:

> Victims need social acknowledgement and support; the court requires them to endure a public challenge to their credibility.

---

[63] J Herman, 'Justice From the Victim's Perspective' (2006) 11 *Violence Against Women* 571 at 574–75.

Courts require testimony or evidence from victims when the matter is contested, that is when the defendant pleads not guilty. If the person charged with the offence admits guilt (which is what happens in the vast majority of matters in magistrates' courts and a significant proportion of matters in higher courts) then there is no challenge to the credibility of the victim. Restorative justice programs also require an admission of the offence by the offender— they are not testing evidence and determining guilt. The point is that those matters where the offender denies committing an offence and where the evidence of the victim is likely to be essential in securing a conviction will not go into a restorative justice program.

> Victims need to establish a sense of power and control over their lives; the court requires them to submit to a complex set of rules and bureaucratic procedures that they may not understand and over which they have no control.

On the face of it legal processes appear bureaucratic and rulebound compared to what is offered by restorative justice. While restorative justice offers greater informality and the rules of evidence are relaxed, it would be a mistake to see restorative justice simply as an ungoverned process. As restorative justice has become increasingly institutionalised, particularly in the area of juvenile justice, so have the legal and bureaucratic requirements surrounding the administration and operation of specific programs. Restorative justice places requirements on victims and offenders. Meeting specific requirements can be subject to potential judicial scrutiny (for example, the failure to meet the requirements of a conference can lead to subsequent court proceedings). One result of the incorporation of restorative justice into traditional justice systems is increased legal and administrative requirements about access, process and outcomes. All of these requirements mould and mediate the experience of victims. Victims do not control the processes and procedures of restorative justice.

> Victims need an opportunity to tell their stories in their own way, in a setting of their choice; the court requires them to respond to a set of

yes-or-no questions that break down any personal attempt to construct a coherent and meaningful narrative.

Legal rules do construct particular narratives, and the narratives demanded by prosecutors and defence lawyers are designed to fulfil certain functions. Rules of evidence may appear somewhat capricious; yet we should remember that rules governing admissibility—requirements of relevance and use of best evidence, prohibitions against hearsay and self-incrimination, and protections for vulnerable witnesses—are there for reasons most people would support: to ensure fairness and to protect against the arbitrary use of state power. Victims themselves are required to present a narrative and be subject to cross-examination only in contested matters (ie the matters that are not likely to find themselves in a restorative justice program). There is perhaps a greater opportunity for a victim to present a meaningful personal account within a restorative justice process, but I also think this can be overstated. Restorative justice programs follow particular scripts which are not controlled by the victim, and it would appear that there is great potential for misreading within the communicative processes of restorative justice. Differing perceptions of the sincerity of apologies are testimony to this problem.[64]

> Victims often need to control or limit their exposure to specific reminders of the trauma; the court requires them to relive the experience. Victims often fear direct confrontation with their perpetrators; the court requires a face-to-face confrontation between a complaining witness and the accused.

As previously noted, in the majority of matters before the courts the victim will not have to relive his or her experience by giving a personal account, although if he or she attends court he or she will hear an account of events by both the prosecutor and the defence, and possibly also by the offender. By way of contrast, restorative justice demands that if a victim attends a program then he or she will be required to face the offender and to re-live the experience.

---

[64] Daly, above n 53.

Even if, in the restorative justice program, the victim chooses not to give a personal account of the impact of the offence, the offender will be required to account for and explain his or her actions. The victim will be involved in a far more personalised face-to-face and confronting meeting with the offender than in the traditional courtroom setting.

> For many victims, even a successful legal outcome does not promise much satisfaction because their goals are not congruent with the sanctions that the system imposes. The victim's vision of justice is nowhere represented in the conventional legal system.

Is the victim's vision of justice represented in restorative justice approaches? Does a successful outcome in restorative justice match the needs of the victim? The first point to note is that, according to evaluations of restorative justice, a successful restorative justice outcome can be achieved without the victim being present in a restorative justice program. In both courts and restorative justice programs successful outcomes (as determined by state administrative procedures) seem largely defined in terms of the offender meeting certain requirements. In those restorative justice situations where the victim is not present—and there are many—the convenor can take on a 'representative' role for the victim. Where only a notional victim (the convenor) is present, it would seem to me to be somewhat artificial to claim that real victim satisfaction with the sanction and outcomes has been achieved. It is also worth noting that victims may be required to give up some of their rights to restitution or compensation as part of a restorative justice agreement.

It appears highly contingent whether the vision of justice of those victims who actually attend restorative justice programs will be realised. Research on victims attending youth justice conferencing found that the level of distress experienced by victims impacted on their view of the program. Those victim's experiencing higher degrees of distress were 'far more likely to remain angry and fearful of offenders and to be negative toward them'.[65] Three-quarters of those who had exhibited high distress at the time of the restorative

---

[65] *Ibid*, at 141.

justice program had not recovered when interviewed 12 months later. They were still more likely to see the offender as a bad person and, importantly, were 'more likely to say they wished their case had gone to court'.[66]

The relationship between victims and offenders also occurs within particular cultural contexts. On the one hand, a meeting between the victim and offender is held to be central to a successful restorative justice reintegration ceremony.[67] Yet despite the claims of connections between indigenous cultures and restorative justice, the processes of resolving disputes in indigenous communities can be far more complex than face-to-face meetings. For example, Blagg has noted the extent to which indigenous societies in Australia seek to avoid open conflict between victim and offender, although such a meeting is at the heart of restorative justice processes.[68] Support for this view can be found in careful and extensive analysis of dispute management in Aboriginal communities such as that undertaken by Williams.[69] Rather than some simplistic process of shaming, she discusses a variety of sanctions used by Yolgnu people in Arnhemland, including temporary exile, temporary internal exile, withdrawal and restitution.[70] Many of these sanctions are clearly based on avoidance rather than confrontation. Similarly, elder groups dealing with indigenous young people in Northern Queensland still rely on various forms of exile through the use of outstations. In central Australia, managing disputes and preparing for the intervention of the non-indigenous criminal justice system may involve complex arrangements between various clan groups conducted in the absence of the offender or the victim.[71]

---

[66] Ibid, *at* 142.

[67] J Braithwaite and S Mugford, 'Conditions of Successful Reintegration Ceremonies' (1994) 34 *British Journal of Criminology* 139.

[68] H Blagg, 'Restorative Visions and Restorative Justice Practices: Conferencing, Ceremony and Reconciliation in Australia' (1998) 10 *Current Issues in Criminal Justice* 5.

[69] N Williams, *Two Laws, Managing Disputes in a Contemporary Aboriginal Community* (Canberra, Australian Institute of Aboriginal Studies, 1987).

[70] *Ibid*, at 96–106.

[71] Cunneen, above n 58.

D. The Offender

Despite the simple vision of the offender in restorative justice literature, it is clear there are very significant differences between offenders and their potential participation in restorative justice programs. One major problem is that of voluntariness. How free are the offenders who participate in restorative justice programs? One of the foundational premises of restorative justice is that the parties need to participate voluntarily. To some extent victims can 'vote with their feet' by refusing to attend. However, the situation is not necessarily the same for offenders. In the UK the Crime and Disorder Act 1998 introduced a form of coercive restorative justice where courts could make reparation orders even where the youth involved did not want it, or in cases where the victim had not been consulted. This authoritarian approach to restorative justice was superseded by the referral order under the Youth Justice and Criminal Evidence Act 1999, which again served as a form of coercive restorative justice.[72]

Coercion in restorative justice can occur on many levels and may be far less overt than found in the UK legislation, which involves legal compulsion. One of the benefits of restorative justice is said to be that it encourages admissions by offenders. Yet this is a double-edged sword. The pressures placed on young people to make admissions regarding an offence so as to avoid court and gain access to a restorative justice program can raise questions about the voluntariness of the processes and the attitudes and expectations of those who attend. Coercion to admit an offence also throws into question the claim that is made that restorative justice is involved only with the penalty stage of the criminal justice system, and that it is distinctly separate from the investigatory and fact-finding stages of the criminal justice process. This claim fails to acknowledge that police can be involved *in practice* in the process of determining guilt through coercive tactics designed to force an individual to admit an offence, and be indirectly involved in admin-

[72] Williams, above n 56.

istering penalty through determining pathways in and out of the criminal justice system. As discussed further at section IV below, police directly determine access to most restorative justice programs, particularly those available for young people. The particular vulnerability of young people during police questioning, and the promise of diversion to a restorative justice program, should alert us to the possibility that the admission of an offence can be coerced.

Given that many offenders who participate in restorative justice programs are young people, we also need to be aware of the impact their age and level of maturity may have on the expected outcomes. Research from South Australia indicated that 27 per cent of young people who apologised did not feel sorry for their victim but thought they would 'get off more easily'. Others apologised to make their own families feel better, and a high proportion also felt 'pushed into it'.[73] This is not to deny that many offenders feel genuinely sorry for what they have done—although their apologies may not be accepted as sincere from some victims. The role of the apology is fundamental to the restorative justice process, particularly where there is a victim present. Yet we know from the existing research that the act of the apology and its reception involve a complex interaction. We demand this from young people who are vulnerable and may not have the capacity to engage fully with the expected outcomes.

Successful restorative justice programs require effective communication. Offenders need to be able to provide good narrative accounts of their offending and their remorse. This is a prerequisite for successfully navigating through the justice system, irrespective of whether we are talking about restorative justice, courts, therapeutic programs or parole hearings. Yet the evidence suggests that young offenders in particular do poorly in this area: learning and other disabilities, mental illness, drug and alcohol abuse are all likely to impact negatively on language abilities, and in particular on the ability to adjust communicative styles to meet differing contexts.

[73] Day, above n 53, at 140.

Narratives form an important part of everyday life, but the research on young offenders suggests they lack the skills to provide adequate narratives which relay their own experiences and feelings, particularly in an unfamiliar social context. These problems can be further exacerbated if the restorative justice program is in a language other than the first language of the offender, or if the offender speaks a dialect of the program language. As noted with Aboriginal youth, problems communicating in what linguists refer to as standard English can result in silence among participants. The outcome can be that the silence is interpreted as sullenness, disregard or disrespect. The end result is that the victim feels more anger and the young offender feels alienated.[74]

I am not suggesting that traditional court processes provide better opportunities for defendants or victims to produce narrative accounts of the crime and its context. However, I am suggesting that the idea that restorative justice programs can offer a 'dialogic encounter' between victims, offenders and supporters is overstated. Although both offenders and victims *may* get to tell their stories, there are also various reasons why neither party may be able to participate effectively in the process. Some of these factors will relate to the institutional setting, the expectations of a set script, and the role of players such as convenors and police. Other factors will include both the offender's and victim's abilities to communicate within the particular context, which is likely to be unfamiliar to both parties.

A great deal of discussion of the victim–offender relationship in restorative justice has rested on the assumption, which is valid in the majority of cases, that the offender will be male. However, the offender may be a woman or, in juvenile conferencing programs, a young woman. Feminist writers have shown that women's behaviour is significantly judged, controlled and disciplined through the criminal justice system. The question which arises is whether we can assume that informal processing through restorative justice

---

[74] M Dodson, *Aboriginal and Torres Strait Islander Social Justice Commissioner Fourth Report* (Canberra, Australian Government Printer Service, 1996).

programs will necessarily be more benign. Why should informal justice processes be any less likely than formal ones to judge girls according to 'limited visions of what is appropriate behaviour for girls'?[75] The evidence from feminist analysis suggests that offending behaviour by women and girls is less accepted by the community, and by both their male and female peers, than similar behaviour by males. Offending by girls and women challenges their status and value as such, and has a significantly negative impact for their sense of identity and self-worth.

The focus in restorative justice on 'reintegrative shaming' also has particular ramifications for women. We know that girls and women in the juvenile and adult justice systems tend to feel guilt and shame for their situation, and that self-harm is a particularly gendered response to emotional pain and frustration. Shame has been a powerful tool for control of women. The question remains whether restorative justice programs will simply extend and entrench the dominant gendered definitions of appropriate female behaviour. Research suggests that such gendered expectations extend beyond the victim and the offender to others involved in the process. Cook's observations on fathers and mothers partici-pating in juvenile restorative justice conferences found that the 'cultural scripts' remained intact.[76] Mothers who attended were presumed responsible for their children's behaviour. Fathers who attended were mostly silent and appeared to be inclined 'shrug off' their sons' behaviours. Cook concludes that class, gender and eth-nicity are prisms through which restorative justice conferences operate: '. . . for the most part, the socially constructed categories of difference are not eliminated but instead are used as subtle devices of domination'.[77]

---

[75] See C Alder, 'Young Women Offenders and the Challenge for Restorative Justice' in H Strang and R Braithwaite, *Restorative Justice: Philosophy to Practice* (Dartmouth, Ashgate, 2000).

[76] K Cook, 'Doing difference and accountability in restorative justice conferences' (2006) 10 *Theoretical Criminology* 107.

[77] *Ibid*, at 121.

E. Structural Inequalities and the Offender/Victim Relationship

The least contentious use of restorative justice is dealing with more minor offences involving juveniles which would ordinarily lead to a police warning or caution, or to a minor penalty if the matter proceeded to court. The type of problems associated with this use of restorative justice often involve ensuring that due process principles are not completely ignored, the restorative justice program is not stigmatising, the penalties are not significantly heavier than a court would normally impose and there are safeguards against substantial net-widening. In this context, restorative justice is essentially a juvenile diversionary scheme. Yet advocates have always argued that restorative justice has much greater potential than this. However, its use in relation to serious offences raises range of other problems.[78] In particular, the broader structural inequalities that contextualise the victim–offender relationship become more apparent. I explore this problem through considering two types of crime—violence against women and hate crime— and question the appropriateness of restorative justice in these matters.

1. *Violence against women*

Perhaps the most sustained critique of restorative justice has come from feminists, who have emphasised the lack of understanding of power relations embedded in responses to crimes against women. Consequently, a great deal of discussion has already occurred about whether restorative justice is a suitable response to domestic and family violence. This has affected restorative justice practice to the extent that in some jurisdictions domestic violence may be excluded from restorative justice processes (along with various forms of sexual assault). To my mind, the responses of those who advocate extension of restorative justice to crimes of violence

---

[78] B Hudson, 'Restorative Justice and Gendered Violence' (2002) 42 *British Journal of Criminology* 616.

against women have not been completely convincing. In fact, the main argument supporting extension seems to be the negative one that because the criminal justice system has dealt poorly with domestic and family violence, restorative justice almost by definition will be a preferable response.

The starting point for feminist arguments is that domestic violence is a special type of crime and that the priority of any sort of intervention must be to ensure physical protection for victims, usually women and children.[79] Restorative justice, it is argued, needs to deconstruct generalised notions of crime and recognise the special nature of domestic violence, ie it is typically not an isolated act involving two individuals who are unknown to each other but rather a gendered strategy of control that includes various types of coercive tactics, and that may be part of a patterned cycle of behaviour which includes contrition and apology. Some of the potential benefits of restorative justice do not apply in domestic and family violence cases; for instance, victims may not benefit from meeting with and learning about the offender but may be personally targeted by the offender. Restorative justice's view of crime is based on an offence as a discrete, past event for which reparation can readily be made. It fails to take account of the special characteristics of domestic violence, which typically is about power and control, is commonly recurrent, exhibits cycles of violence and contrition, and may escalate in intensity over time.

Furthermore, there are social and cultural dimensions that give meaning and authorisation to the violence, and constrain women's options in response.[80] We cannot assume that actors marshalled together for a restorative justice conference will be capable of providing the necessary support for victims who are in a structurally disadvantaged position. We know that popular discourses continue to construct women as complicit in domestic violence and to trivialise the offence. We cannot be sure that restorative justice

---

[79] J Stubbs, 'Domestic Violence and Women's Safety: feminist challenges to restorative justice' in H Strang and J Braithwaite (eds), *Restorative Justice and Family Violence* (Cambridge, Cambridge University Press, 2002).

[80] *Ibid*, at 45.

practices will effectively challenge the offender's attempts to control the situation or neutralise responsibility. There is no guarantee, therefore, that a more progressive understanding of domestic violence will emerge through a restorative justice program.[81]

Indeed, the basic premise of restorative justice, that the harm between victim and offender is to be repaired, must be questioned as an outcome sought by women seeking intervention, support and protection against violence. Herman's interviews with survivors of domestic violence and sexual assault showed that women were not interested in revenge or punishment for its own sake; they were also not interested in reconciliation or forgiveness.[82] They preferred exposure of the perpetrator—thereby depriving him of undeserved honour or status—and acknowledgement of them and their story by their communities. Safety for themselves and other potential victims was also sought. The danger with restorative justice is that public denunciation will not occur, and it may encourage women to stay in violent relationships.

Restorative justice was developed with a view to dealing with essentially non-violent offences committed by young people, where there was no stigma attached to the victims and where offenders could be welcomed back into the community as part of the restorative justice process. Herman has noted that in cases of domestic or sexual violence, the person who needs to be welcomed back into the community is the victim.[83] The victims feel shamed and stigmatised by their communities as a result of what has occurred. Herman's interviews revealed that only a minority of women survivors of domestic violence and sexual assault had been able to achieve anything like a satisfactory outcome in relation to the offences in question, *irrespective* of whether they had tried to seek justice formally or informally. Those who went to court were somewhat more successful than those who chose informal methods, but in general both responses were unsatisfactory. Victims said about their encounters

---

[81]   *Ibid.*

[82]   J Herman, 'Justice From the Victim's Perspective' (2006) 11 *Violence Against Women* 571.

[83]   *Ibid.*

with the criminal justice system that they saw 'just how little they mattered'. In informal methods of resolution the victims thought the community and family appeared to be allied to the perpetrators.

There is also the particular context in which minority women face violence. There is no reason to expect that restorative justice practices will privilege, or indeed give a voice to, these women when they seek protection. There may be particular cultural concerns that will influence how immigrant women participate in restorative justice. Goel focuses upon South Asian women in the US, who are 'particularly prone to flawed solutions to battering for many reasons, but most important, cultural ideals exert tremendous pressure to accept less-than-ideal solutions'.[84] She argues in particular that the Indian ideal is self-sacrifice, not self-preservation; and as a result, Indian women may be less easily able to advocate for their own interests in a restorative justice program. While Indian women do not necessarily suffer higher rates of domestic and family violence, immigrant status and cultural difference is likely to affect access to and use of legal responses and relevant services. Idealised and exoticised constructions of South Asian women as law-abiding, hard-working and 'ultra-feminine' can make it more difficult for Indian women to seek assistance.

Restorative justice programs may not be in a position to respond adequately to different groups of women who experience differing levels of violence. In Australia, for example, the homicide rate for indigenous women is 10 times that of other women. Other minority women also have variable rates, for example Filipino women's homicide rate is five times the general rate for other women in Australia.[85] These differences directly reflect the gendered outcomes of colonial and post-colonial conditions. Having said that, it is also worth noting that colonised women's appalling experience

---

[84] R Goel, 'Sita's Trousseau' (2005) 11 *Violence Against Women* 639.

[85] C Cunneen and J Stubbs, 'Migration, Political Economy and Violence Against Women: the post immigration experiences of Filipino women in Australia' in J D Freilich, G Newman, S G Shoham and M Addad (eds), *Migration, Culture Conflict and Crime* (Aldershot, Ashgate, 2002).

with Western criminal justice interventions may lead some to see restorative justice as a potential avenue for better outcomes.[86]

Lastly, we should be concerned about the pressures on victims of domestic violence in particular to participate in restorative justice programs and to reach an 'acceptable' outcome. Certainly some victims may not be able to advocate adequately for themselves within a restorative justice setting. Coker's discussion of Navajo peacemaking in cases of domestic and family violence exemplifies some of the problems of coercion through forcing victim participation. She quotes a worker from a domestic violence program as follows:

> My clients get intimidating letters [from Peacemaker Court] saying they have to come to Peacemaking. The women get really scared. The women are forced to go. I've had two other clients who tried to get out of Peacemaking. One had gone to the shelter and [her partner] filed for Peacemaking. She was really scared. She had left the reservation [to get away from him] and was living in another town. [The] Peacemaking liaison started coming to [the domestic violence program], pushing [staff] to disclose the woman's location. The . . . staff replied that the information was confidential. The [battered] woman asked [the domestic violence program] staff to tell [the] liaison that she didn't want to do this. The liaison kept telling staff that he just wanted to talk with her, that he had to hear from her directly. So the staff recommended that she put her concerns in writing and the staff delivered the letter. Even then the liaison still wanted 'just a few minutes with her'.[87]

Peacemaking's primary response to coercion in the process is to rely upon the peacemaker and the victim's family to stand up for the victim. However, there clearly may be considerable pressure prior to the Peacemaker Court taking place.

---

[86] H Nancarrow, 'In Search of Justice for Domestic and Family Violence: Indigenous and Non-Indigenous Australian Women's Perspectives' (2006) 10 *Theoretical Criminology*. 87.

[87] D Coker, 'Enhancing Autonomy for Battered Women: Lessons from Navajo Peacemaking' (2000) 47 *University of California Law Review* 1.

2. Hate crime

In terms of the relationship between the victim and the offender, hate crime is clearly different from domestic and family violence. It is a stranger crime, at least to the extent that the victim (whether known to the offender or not) is victimised on the basis of his or her representativeness of a racial, ethnic, religious or sexual social group (ie gay, lesbian, Jew, Asian, African). The individual victim is seen as standing for the group which has been categorised as the hated 'other'.

Given the nature of hate crime, particularly the broader social group that supports and defines the hatred by the individual perpetrator, it is at best a high-risk strategy to expect a restorative justice process to change the view of the offender towards the victim. As in cases of domestic and family violence, the broader community and the more immediate social network of which the offender is part may in fact provide support for the offender's action rather than challenge him or her to reflect critically on the harm he or she has caused. The difficulty is that justifications for racist violence and other hate crimes, like justifications for violence against women, may be deeply embedded in cultural values that are not readily challenged in the context of a restorative justice forum. The consensus among the offender's social networks may be that the crime is acceptable, or at least tolerable. The benign and tolerant virtues necessary for restorative justice may be absent. There is no reason why an essentially private restorative justice approach is particularly likely to lead to better outcomes than a traditional criminal justice response, which may involve public denunciation of the offending behaviour.

As in the case of domestic and family violence, it may be a better outcome for the victim for the state to punish the crime and to remove the victim from the responsibility of confronting the perpetrator. Furthermore, hate crime tends to cause harm both to the individual and the broader social group which has been targeted. Public denunciation rather than individual apology may be the most acceptable outcome because it speaks to the broader social group more directly than a private apology to an individual. Those that support the use of restorative justice for hate crime do so on the speculative grounds that the offender can see how his or her offence affected the individual and the relevant community, and that the victim can break down any stereotypes and prejudices of the offender, thus deterring future hate crimes.[88] The latter point in particular seems to involve a perverse form of victim responsibility for changing the offender.

3. Social inequality

Both violence against women and hate crime are closely bound to wider social constructions of gender, sexuality, race and ethnicity. On the one hand it may be the case that law and legal institutions support these forms of violence both in ideology and practice. But recognising this is not an argument in itself for restorative justice. The social and institutional practices that support gendered and racialised violence are not going to disappear because of the relocation of a process from the court to a more informal setting. The struggle to ensure safety, to provide reassurance, to rehabilitate an individual perpetrator all involve commitment, time and resources from a range of social actors. It may that this is better achieved working through a well-coordinated, formalised set of interventions. As Stubbs has noted, one restorative justice meeting is unlikely to change structural inequality and deeply held misogynist or racist views.[89] The potential privatisation of responses to both violence against women and hate crime has a range of potential negative consequences. It runs the risk of silencing the public denunciation of these offences, which for decades now activists have struggled to get on the public agenda. There is no reasonable argument to suggest that restorative justice will be any more likely meaningfully to address the underlying causes of these offences than the criminal justice system. Indeed, there are many reasons to

---

[88] See, eg, A Schenk, 'Victim–Offender Mediation: The Road to Repairing Hate Crime Injustice' (2001) 17 *Ohio State Journal on Dispute Resolution* 185.

[89] Stubbs, above n 79.

think that a restorative justice response will be less able to address structural inequalities because of less public accountability, fewer resources, less access to co-ordinated services and the potential perpetuation of power imbalances.

F. *Victims, Offenders, Rights and Incommensurability*

The last issue I want to address in this discussion of victims and offenders is the problem of incommensurability, particularly where the offender does not believe the actions he or she engaged in were in fact criminal. There is a claim that restorative justice can balance the needs of the offender and victim, and lead to a just reconciliation between the two. Perhaps this is the case in some matters. But it is also the case that the interests of victims and offenders may conflict in many instances, and in more extreme cases may be incommensurable. In these cases the relative impartiality of the criminal justice system is likely to be more effective.

The example provided below is a difficult one because it highlights matters of gender, race, cultural difference and violence against women. This recent case from the Northern Territory of Australia raises concerns about the appropriateness of sanctions and basic definitions of crime, fundamental human rights, and the complexity of developing appropriate social and judicial responses. GJ was a 55-year-old traditional Aboriginal man convicted of assaulting and having unlawful sexual intercourse with a 14-year-old Aboriginal girl. When the child was about 4 years of age, in the traditional way of the Aboriginal law of the community, the Ngarinaman Law, the child was promised as a wife to the older man. The 14-year-old was to be his second wife, and his first wife and their children were to remain as part of the household. In sentencing, Judge Martin noted the following:

> This is an extremely difficult case . . . You believed that traditional law permitted you to strike the child and to have intercourse with her. On the other hand, the law of the Northern Territory says that you cannot hit a child. The law of the Northern Territory also says that you cannot have intercourse with a child . . .

You and the child's grandmother decided that you would take the child to your outstation. The grandmother told you to take the child and the grandmother told the child that she had to go with you. The child did not want to go with you and told you she did not want to go. The child also asked her grandmother if she could stay. Rather than help the child, the grandmother packed personal belongings for her . . .

The child later told the police that she was 'at that old man's place for four days', and that she was crying 'from Saturday to Tuesday'. She knew that she was promised to you in the Aboriginal traditional way, but she did not like you. In the words of the child, 'I told that old man I'm too young for sex, but he didn't listen.'[90]

GJ admitted hitting the child with a boomerang and having sexual intercourse with the child. He told police that in Aboriginal culture the child was promised as a wife from the time she was 4 years old, and said that it was acceptable to start having sexual intercourse with a girl when she was 14 years old. It was clear that the child's grandmother was also influential in ensuring that the child submitted to what was seen as a traditional marriage. Judge Martin noted:

I appreciate that it is a very difficult thing for men who have been brought up in traditional ways which permit physical violence and sexual intercourse with promised wives, even if they are not consenting, to adjust their ways. But it must be done. I hope that by sitting in your community today and saying these words, and I hope that by the sentence that I am going to impose upon you, that the message will get out not just to your community, but to communities across the Territory . . .

You have had a strong ceremonial life across widespread communities. You are regarded by the Yarralin Community as an important person in the ceremonial life of the community. You are responsible for teaching young men the traditional ways. I accept that these offences occurred because the young child had been promised to you . . .[91]

---

[90] *Queen v GJ*, Supreme Court of Northern Territory, SCC 20418849, 11 August 2005, Martin CJ, at 1–2.

[91] *Ibid*, at 3–4.

In this case the community of the elder was not likely to challenge the behaviour of someone who was essentially following the law of the community. Despite offending against the dominant law of the state, the elder was not offending against local law under which he lived most of his life. It is precisely the type of case which is not likely to find resolution within a community-based restorative just-ice framework—indeed, within that framework there would have been no case to answer. In this case the traditional criminal justice system can respond in a way which denounces the offence, and can attempt to provide a reintegrative sentence by acknowledging that the elder acted within his own cultural beliefs rather than out of an intentional act of sexual violence:

> I have spoken quite a lot about what you believed and how you felt. I must also remind you about how the child felt. She was upset and dis-tressed and I have no doubt that your act of intercourse with her has had a significant effect upon her. The child has provided only a very brief Victim Impact Statement in which she does not speak of any emotional and psychological impact upon her. That is not surprising. This is a child who has been shamed within a community that obviously has very strong male members and strong traditional beliefs. It is not surprising that she would not be prepared to publicly state how she was feeling. I do not know, therefore, the extent of the effects or how long they will last, but I have no doubt that the effects have been significant.[92]

The case shows how unlikely it would have been for the young victim to participate effectively in a restorative justice conference. She was shamed in the community where traditional beliefs did not condemn the violence to which she had been subjected. In this case the criminal justice system is able to denounce the criminal behav-iour and vindicate the victim in way that could not have occurred in a more informal community-based setting. Both the community and the family of the victim upheld the right of the offender to take the actions he had, and would have been unlikely to see the young woman as a victim of crime.

[92] *Ibid*, at 4.

Some commentators have argued for a rights-based approach to restorative justice that acknowledges the rights of the victim and the offender, that acknowledges that these rights may be in conflict, and that specifies what should happen in these cases where rights are in conflict.[93] The theory is that it is sometimes morally possible to subjugate one person's rights upon the basis of another's 'competing rights'. An offender's right to freedom(s) might thus be diminished to repair the harm done to the victim's right to freedom from physical or psychological pain. The problem is more complex in the example given above, where broader community standards (including internationally recognised human rights for women and children) are in conflict with traditional law and local community beliefs. In these cases, specific law is part of the problem where it conflicts with broader standards. The case shows that we cannot assume consensus on what constitutes lawful and unlawful behaviour. There is clearly significant support among GJ's community for traditional law to be upheld. In these matters a formal judicial response compliant with international standards would appear to be far more beneficial than a community-based restorative justice program.

This section of the essay has provided a critique of restorative justice on the basis of our understanding of the victims and offenders. It has argued for a more nuanced approach which does not see these categories as simple binary opposites. There is a range of victim responses to crime and to offenders. Some victims will be deeply affected, others will not; some will desire to confront the offender, others would prefer to have no contact. For victims who are deeply distressed, restorative justice can have negative outcomes. Despite the apparent centrality of victims to the theory, in practice much restorative justice occurs without a victim being present. Coercion can be a real problem for both offenders and victims. Miscommunication and limited abilities to provide narrative accounts make the outcomes of the process less clear-cut for both

---

[93] J Dignan, *Understanding Victims and Restorative Justice* (Maidenhead, Open University Press, 2005) 179–83.

parties. Part of the commonsense appeal of restorative justice is the way it produces understandings of victims and offenders as unambiguous and uncomplicated individuals. It reproduces ideas and knowledge about criminal offending and about victimisation. Yet the social reality is far more complex. Inequality and power do not disappear simply because of a change in the legal forum: gender, race, class and ethnicity continue to structure the ways individuals experience justice. Neither offending nor victimisation arise outside of these broader social relations.

IV. LAW, STATE AND COMMUNITY

The relationship between restorative justice and law, the state and the community is complex. I want to use this last section of the essay to explore some of the failings of restorative justice within this broad arena. They include the inability of restorative justice effectively to articulate a relationship to law and a broader theory of state power. Criminal justice systems, of which restorative justice is now one part, have moved towards far more punitive outcomes for offenders over the last several decades, giving rise in particular to the phenomenon of mass imprisonment. While it may be convenient to paint restorative justice as an approach outside of this trend, it seems more plausible to consider how restorative justice has been articulated within a growing acceptance of treating both juvenile and adult offending populations more harshly. More punitive criminal justice responses have occurred at the same time as processes such as restorative justice have allowed a greater level of governance through reliance on the 'community' as a part of justice strategies. Lastly, I comment on the growth of restorative justice as a strategy in transitional societies, which I argue highlights the complexity of the relationship between state and community.

A. The Role of Law and the State

The construction of restorative justice by its advocates appears to make law and the state take a largely diminished role, if not completely disappear. Indeed, the rhetorical delimitation of restorative justice is in opposition to law (crime is a harm to the victim, not just the community; procedural rules of evidence are oppressive) and the state (the state does not represent the interests of the victim, the state is only interested in retribution; the state 'steals' community conflicts). It is fair to ask, then, 'Where is law?' and 'Where is the state in restorative justice?'. If we look critically, we see that both law and the state permeate restorative justice completely. And this is the paradox that restorative justice faces. While restorative justice presents itself as outside law to the extent that it is an alternative to the legal processes of sentencing and punishment, it is also regulated by law; and while it presents itself outside the state, it is dependent upon state institutions, including the police, the courts, and juvenile and adult correctional facilities, for its legal subjects and the legitimation of its own processes.

Law frames restorative justice in the most basic sense of determining those acts and actors upon which restoration may take place. Law defines its subjects. Law delineates, categorises and constitutes the groups of offenders who can be diverted into restorative processes and those who are beyond the pale (eg violent offenders, sex offenders, repeat offenders), and those offences which can and cannot be determined through a restorative process. As we noted in the discussion of victims (section III. above), law has an interpellative function calling into being legal subjects. This is an important element in understanding the problem restorative justice has in reimagining the victim and the offender as individuals simultaneously embedded in social relationships. In the first instance one can only participate in a restorative practice as a legal subject called into being by the law—I am a self-confessed and repentant offender; I am a forgiving victim. Once in a restorative justice meeting, the offender is removed from the earlier criminalisation processes—he or she is no longer the young person targeted by the police because he or she is black; the homeless arrested because of his or her threat to public order; or the mentally ill person criminalised because of the absence of other support systems.

Further, law constructs schedules of offences, according to their seriousness and the harm they inflict, on the basis of which the criminal justice system may or may not relinquish responsibility for formal prosecution and punishment. Restorative justice as a practice operates on those offences and offenders deemed suitable by law. Law also delimits the outer boundaries of restitution, reparation and punishment. For example, circle sentencing in Canada and Aboriginal courts in Australia provide opportunities for community participants to provide advice to judicial officers on appropriate sentences. However, these special courts are part of the wider criminal justice system, and result in convictions and criminal records for offenders. The ultimate sentencing decision lies with the judge, who is free to ignore the sentencing circle or Aboriginal court recommendations, and who is obliged to impose a 'fit' sentence which is still subject to appellate court sentencing guidelines or review. While at one level circle sentencing and Aboriginal courts are held out as examples of restorative justice, they are also constrained by the wider powers of the criminal justice system.

Restorative justice is not without law or outside law. Having said that, part of the paradox is that restorative justice can also been seen in the context of a dispersal of power away from more formal legal institutions and into processes which facilitate greater levels of citizen or community participation. Power is also constitutive, positively forming and moulding social practice. Despite the location of restorative practices in the community, the law still confers power on various participants, from the police officers in a youth justice conference through to the court which may be involved in monitoring the successful outcome of a conference or other restorative practice. Law still maintains the authority of these institutions to define and determine criminal behaviour, while through restorative justice law potentially achieves more direct penetration and greater dispersal into civil society. Restorative justice assists in legitimising state institutions by naturalising their presence in a community setting.

What role does restorative justice play in securing the broader hegemony of law and power through its apparently human face? As Coker has noted, despite the restorative justice view of the state as some distant or irrelevant actor, state power 'suffuses all criminal justice processes', including restorative justice.[94] The law is involved in defining what constitutes an offence, and state actors within the criminal justice system determine 'how these laws are applied, to whom, and under what circumstances'. Restorative justice legitimates state power 'through reinforcing behavioural norms reflected in the laws and through naturalizing the justice practices that bring the offender to the attention of the restorative process'.[95]

It may be argued that restorative justice secures the hegemony of law by making the harsher aspects of the criminal justice system more palatable, particularly its racialised, gendered and class-based effects, and the significant growth in human warehousing in overcrowded prisons we have witnessed over the last several decades. Coercion and consent are connected strategies in maintaining hegemony. An understanding of this connection is important for seeing how restorative justice fits within broader patterns of the coercive powers of the state. For example, in many western jurisdictions restorative justice exists inside the legal and administrative frameworks of criminal justice, which include increased police powers, anti-social behaviour orders, parenting orders, curfews, public naming and shaming of offenders, the loss of presumption in favour of release on bail, offender registries, mandatory sentencing and three-strikes legislation, preventive and indefinite detention, longer periods of incarceration, and an inexorable rise in adult and juvenile prison numbers. The list of clearly non-restorative interventions could go on. The point is that an effective analysis of restorative justice requires that it be seen within the broader strategies in place for the operation of the criminal justice system, and

---

 [94] D Coker, 'Transformative justice: anti-subordination processes in cases of domestic violence' in Strang and Braithwaite, above n 79.

[95] *Ibid,*

these broader strategies have been mainly coercive in their focus, not restorative.

A critical analysis of restorative justice and its relationship to state power is not new. At the same time as emerging restorative justice practices, particularly in juvenile justice, were being formulated in the early 1990s, lawyers and criminologists were also raising the problem of the relationship between restorative justice and the state.[96] In particular, the developing state control of restorative justice appeared to undermine its more radical potential. It appeared that the claims of many restorative justice advocates embodied both a profound naivety about the nature of politics and a sanguine view of state power. As White argued, restorative justice

> accepts at face value the liberal democratic notion that the state is somehow neutral and above sectional interests, that it operates for the 'common good', and that it is an impartial and independent arbiter of conflicts.[97]

There has been little recognition by restorative justice proponents of the move over the past two decades from a social state to a more repressive state as part of the ascendancy of neo-liberal politics. The withdrawal from responsibility in areas of health, education and welfare, and the shift towards modes of governance through privatisation, and individual and community responsibilisation, have all had profound effects on the role of the state in crime control. Similarly, the class-based impact of unemployment and marginalisation, particularly among young people, poses very real problems for restorative justice practice—especially if that practice is built on a presumption of individualised responsibility for crime and restoration. Restorative justice practice must respond seriously to these broader social and economic issues, and it must be able to deal constructively with the various 'hidden injuries' of class,

---

[96] R White, 'Shaming and Reintegrative Strategies: individuals, state power and social interests' in C Alder and J Wundersitz (eds), *Family Conferencing and Juvenile Justice: the way forward or misplaced optimism?* (Canberra, Australian Institute of Criminology, 1994).

[97] *Ibid*, at 187.

including alienation from school and work, homelessness, drug abuse and marginalisation.

The relationship of restorative justice to the state also poses a number of theoretical problems. Braithwaite has suggested that we have seen three types of state formations over the last two centuries: first, the nightwatchman state, where most of the steering and rowing[98] was done by civil society; secondly, the Keynesian state, where the state did a lot of rowing but was weak on steering civil society; and, thirdly, the new regulatory state, where the ideal is the state concentrating on steering while civil society is rowing.[99] The new regulatory state has involved privatisation and 'responsibilisation'—where individuals are required to be responsible for their own welfare and interests. According to Braithwaite, as the state has withdrawn from 'rowing', it has set up regulators to ensure that the public interest is protected. The development of restorative justice is an important part of the new regulatory state in the criminal justice arena—people are required to resolve their own conflicts with guidance from state-appointed facilitators and mediators. In discussing Braithwaite's argument, Bottoms raises a fundamental question: if the analysis is correct, why does restorative justice arise in predominantly managerialist societies with control-orientated penal systems (in which the state appears to be doing all the rowing)?[100] The answer to this question is that the regulatory state may have a dual focus in the criminal justice area: a coercive, risk-focused state criminal justice system for more serious and persistent criminality, and a 'delegation to local communities of the process of dealing with non-persistent, low level criminality'.[101] What flows from this point is that we need to understand the development of mass imprisonment and punitive law-and-order politics as part of a broadly bifurcated approach that

[98] The 'steering' and 'rowing' metaphors are used by Braithwaite to capture differing state activities of engagement directly in enterprise and service provision (rowing) to leading, directing or guiding various economic and social goals (steering).

[99] J Braithwaite, 'The New Regulatory State and the Transformation of Criminology' (2000) 40 *British Journal of Criminology* 222.

[100] Bottoms, above n 15.

[101] *Ibid*, at 108.

also allows for more informal and less-punitive approaches, like restorative justice, to co-exist at the margins of the system.

B. Policing and Criminalisation

There is a great deal of literature on the problems of police discretionary decision-making, the ways in which police decisions impact on an individual's entry into and progression through the criminal justice system, and the manner in which police decision-making is influenced by the social dynamics of race, class and gender. In many jurisdictions the police exercise significant discretionary powers over restorative justice programs. For example, police can determine access to youth justice conferencing programs, and play a key role in the operation of the restorative justice conferencing process and subsequent agreements. The police played an instrumental role in establishing many of the initial restorative justice programs in Australia and the UK.

The centrality of the police role in restorative justice practices is especially problematic given concerns over the inappropriate exercise of police discretion, the dominance of police and other professionals over conference participants, and the lack of accountability of the police. The expanded police role in restorative justice programs has coincided with significant legislative extensions of police powers in a range of other areas, from anti-social behavioural orders and increased stop-and-search powers, particularly affecting young people, to the raft of anti-terrorist legislation introduced since 2001. In most jurisdictions, the increased role of police has not been accompanied by any increases in accountability or control over police decision-making, either specifically in regard to restorative justice or in more general terms. These greater powers have the effect of bringing more people into all areas of the criminal justice system, including those deemed 'restorative'. What we are seeing here is not simply 'net-widening', but rather a substantial increase in both the regulatory *and* coercive powers of the state.

Policing and the criminal justice system have a determining role in constituting social groups as threats and in reproducing a society built on racialised, gendered and class-based boundaries. The process of criminalisation plays a significant part in the reproduction of social marginalisation. Increased police powers, public order interventions over minor offences, the discriminatory use of stop-and-searches based on race, are as much part of the fabric of policing as restorative justice. Racial, ethnic and indigenous minorities may have good reason to be sceptical that police are independent arbiters in the process of restorative justice. Certainly there is the danger that minority youth will be classified by police as 'unsuitable' for restorative justice schemes, particularly if they have prior offending histories or are deemed uncooperative. The empirical evidence shows that minority youth are much less likely to be dealt with via diversionary options such as restorative justice, and are more likely to be processed through the most punitive avenues available.[102] Indeed, colonised peoples and minority populations may simply fail to accept the legitimacy of state-sponsored restorative justice programs—they may be viewed with suspicion and seen as another element of criminalisation and control.

In the youth justice area, the advent of restorative justice has simply seen an added 'alternative' provided to police in responding to young people. However, the use of this alternative is within a system which is largely split between the availability of softer, more community-orientated approaches for some offenders and more punitive pro-arrest strategies for the majority of those who come into contact with the criminal justice system. At the same time as restorative justice pilot projects were being developed by the police, there was the far more widespread use of zero-tolerance policing strategies. These approaches relied heavily on targeting low-level offenders, mapping hot spots, the statistical profiling of particular crimes and likely offenders, the identification and surveillance of recidivists, and the use of pro-arrest strategies and of

---

[102] C Cunneen and R White, *Juvenile Justice: Youth and Crime in Australia*, 3rd edn (Melbourne, Oxford University Press, 2007).

more heavily restricted bail and supervision conditions. These more coercive initiatives have also fitted well with neo-liberal approaches to public-sector managerialism and the demands for risk assessment, targeted use of resources, performance indicators and measurable outcomes.[103] A differentiated response to crime which is based on risk analysis is seen as better use of scarce resources than applying the same criminal justice intervention to all offenders. In this context, the development of restorative justice is not anomalous; it provides a response by police to those offenders who are classified as low-risk. Far from having the potential of providing a radical alternative to contemporary criminal justice practice, restorative justice simply became part of established police practice of selectively classifying and dividing troublesome populations.

C. Punishment and Risk

Restorative justice reaches into longstanding debates about the nature and purpose of punishment. Advocates have portrayed restorative justice as a contrary approach to retributivist or rehabilitation models of justice. However, research on restorative justice practices, such as that conducted by Daly, suggests that in reality, restorative justice combines elements of both retribution and rehabilitation.[104] In other words, a particular practice can combine multiple penal objectives—even if on the face of it these objectives appear to be contradictory or in conflict. Perhaps more significantly, restorative justice programs have been introduced within a framework of greater emphasis on individual responsibility, deterrence and incapacitation. As is widely acknowledged, there has been a significant intensification of punishment over the past

---

[103] C Cunneen, 'The Political Resonance of Crime Control Strategies: Zero Tolerance Policing' in R Hil and G Tait (eds), *Hard Lessons. Reflections on Governance and Crime Control in Late Modernity* (Aldershot, Ashgate, 2004).

[104] Daly, above n 2; Daly, above n 53; K Daly, 'A tale of two studies: RJ from a victim's perspective' in E Elliot and R Gordon (eds), *New Directions in RJ: Issues, Practice, Evaluation* (Devon, Willan Publishing, 2005).

decades—at the same time as restorative justice practices have been introduced. Thus there may be elements of restorative justice, retribution, just deserts, rehabilitation and incapacitation all operating within a particular jurisdiction at any one time. Indeed, in states where restorative justice has been introduced through legislation, it is not unusual to find politicians contextualising these changes as part of a move away from 'leniency' to increased accountability and more severe penalties for offenders.

Discussions of postmodern penality are useful in contextualising the place of restorative justice in contemporary fields of punishment. Pratt, for example, has discussed the return of public shaming, and the resurfacing of a pre-modern penal quality.[105] He also notes the development of other phenomena that would seem out of place within a modern penal framework, including boot camps, curfews and the abandonment of proportionality.[106] O'Malley has discussed the 'bewildering array' of developments in penal policy, including policies based on discipline, punishment, enterprise, incapacitation, restitution and reintegration—policies which are mutually incoherent and contradictory but which co-exist with particular penal regimes.[107] For example, juvenile justice systems within a single jurisdiction can operate with work orders, boot camps, restorative justice conferences between victims and offenders, and three-strikes mandatory imprisonment for certain types of offences. Restorative justice claims of moral certainty and offender responsibility fit well with politicians who acclaim the ability to shame offenders publicly through a range of techniques from the public naming of young offenders to the use of chain gangs and other forms of contemporary public identification of adult offenders. Braithwaite's distinction between reintegrative and disintegrative shaming may provide a moral and ethical escape for

---

[105] J Pratt, D Brown, S Hallsworth, and W Morrison (eds), *The New Punitiveness. Trends, Theories, Perspectives* (Uffculme, Willan Publishing, 2005). Penal modernism is taken to refer to principles based on a scientific approach to punishment including both proportionality in punishment and the rehabilitation of the offender. A 'pre-modern' penality can be said to emphasise public humiliation, shaming and retribution.

[106] *Ibid*, at 131–33.

[107] O'Malley, above n 40.

academics who wish to distance themselves from harsh practices which claim to be restorative. However, it does little to assist with understanding the political imperative to make offenders publicly pay for their sins, and the subsequent popularity of the 'shaming' element of restorative justice.

The movement of penal regimes towards greater reliance on the prediction of risk has been identified since the early work of Feeley and Simon on the development of 'techniques for identifying, classifying and managing groups assorted by dangerousness'.[108] The emphasis on actuarialism, the prediction of risk and policies of incapacitation is not contradictory to the development of restorative justice practices; rather, the two can be seen as complementary strategies within penal regimes. Indeed, risk assessment becomes a fundamental technique in dividing populations between those who benefit from restorative justice practices and those who are channelled into more punitive processes of incapacitation through being refused bail, or facing mandatory supervision or imprisonment. Risk is increasingly assessed using a variety of 'weak' and 'strong' risk-predictive mechanisms, from a simple recognition of prior criminal record through to the application of specifically designed risk assessment tools. The assessment of risk certainly does not take place only in the sentencing stage—indeed in many jurisdictions it may have only limited application at that stage. As noted previously, risk assessment technologies form the core of zero-tolerance policing approaches through the identification of 'hot spots', the statistical profiling of particular crimes and criminals, and so on. Weaker forms of risk assessment may permeate other levels of decision-making: for example, access to bail or access to diversionary options on the basis of prior offending history, failure to comply with previous court orders, etc. Statistically robust risk assessment tools, like the Youth Service Level Case Management Inventory used in countries such as Canada and Australia, apply a veneer of science to the sorting of people (often

[108] M Feeley and J Simon, 'Actuarial Justice: the emerging new criminal law' in D Nelken (ed), *The Futures of Criminology* (London, Sage, 1994) 173.

on the basis of race and class) for a variety of purposes, including access to restorative justice programs. The focus on individual factors, such as the age of the offender when first receiving a court order, prior record, prior failures to comply with orders and current offences, is used to predict risk of future offending. Various socio-economic factors are also connected to risk, including education (eg 'problematic' schooling and truancy) and unemployment. The individual 'risk' factors are de-contextualised from wider social and economic constraints. Through the miracle of statistics, the most marginalised groups within society reappear as those who present the greatest risk to security. The ascendancy of 'evidence-based' research tells us that these are the 'problem cases' unlikely to respond to the opportunities offered by restorative justice, and are fit subjects for more restrictive and coercive law-and-order policies.

We can see the processes of risk assessment operating more clearly in the environment of a greater *bifurcation* of existing justice systems. Restorative justice conferencing models have been introduced in a context where juvenile justice systems are increasingly responding to two categories of offenders: those defined as 'minor', and those who are seen as serious or repeat offenders. Minor offenders benefit from various diversionary programs such as restorative justice schemes. Serious and repeat offenders, on the other hand, are ineligible for diversionary programs and are dealt with more punitively through sentencing regimes that are more akin to adult models, ie with a greater preparedness to use imprisonment in matters that might previously have attracted a non-custodial sentence, provisions for mandatory minimum terms of imprisonment for some categories of offences (for example, repeat property offences) and indeterminate sentences for some categories of offenders (for example, sex offenders). It is not surprising, in these circumstances, that we have seen very significant rises in the incarceration rates of young people precisely at the same time as youth offending rates have stabilised or begun to fall, and precisely in those nations, like the US, Australia, Canada, the UK and New Zealand, where restorative justice programs have been introduced with great fanfare. In most of these cases, restorative justice programs have been established within broader public policy frameworks that have emphasised individual responsibility and accountability, public denunciation of offenders, deterrence and incapacitation.

Punishment in late modern societies incorporates a variety of goals and processes, from restorative justice to incapacitation.[109] While bifurcation is a useful way of seeing the separation between restorative justice and the more punitive developments in criminal justice policy and practice, it is important to acknowledge that the bifurcation is asymmetrical. In other words, restorative justice is very much the junior partner in the changes that have unfolded. Further, these processes of asymmetrical bifurcation have been intensifying over the past decade or so, particularly with changes in bail and sentencing legislation. The overall effect of penal policy has been a substantial increase in more punitive outcomes.[110] In this context, restorative justice is reduced to yet another penal strategy reserved for those who are deserving, while the 'undeserving' (the homeless, the marginalised, the poor and non-white populations) receive what they have always received—imprisonment, but now in ever-increasing numbers. Restorative justice is part of the wide-ranging politics of a new period of 'mass imprisonment'.[111] This change represents a reversal of earlier trends, where prison rates had been relatively stable or increasing only slowly during most of the twentieth century. According to many commentators, the rise of mass imprisonment is consistent with the broader political agenda of the neo-liberal state, a move away from rehabilitative aims and an increased reliance on risk assessment. This transformation in penality has seen changes in the ideas, practices and sensibilities of punishment, and a revalorisation of the prison. My

---

[109] I am using 'late modern societies' to refer to highly developed, technologically advanced and mostly western nations where crime and uncertainty are major components of public life. Specifically in regard to penality, the modernist project of scientific reformation of the offender remains but is overladen with a range of pre-modern penal goals.

[110] Pratt *et al*, above n 105.

[111] Garland, above n 7.

ıment is that restorative justice is contextualised by this wider ısformation and valorisation of punitive punishments. Prison not only 'works', it works so well that we can have effective restorative justice within prison. And indeed, according to some, we can have effective restorative justice in capital punishment cases prior to execution—in what appears as an extraordinarily counter-intuitive understanding of the possibilities of restoration.[112]

D. The Community

Restorative justice theory assumes, and restorative justice practice requires, the existence of community. Community appears in restorative justice as the 'spontaneous and voluntary collective domains that constitute the foundations of civil society'.[113] Restorative justice proponents have attempted to answer the question of whether community exists in late modern society by suggesting that there are increased levels of interdependency in globalised societies, and that while geographic communities may have declined, non-geographic 'communities of fate' have replaced them. Finally, among all individuals some vestige of community can be found and built upon.

Bottoms has, among many others, questioned whether there are adequate 'meso-social structures' to support a restorative justice approach.[114] Society is no longer full of the 'thick' social relationships required by restorative justice. Although perhaps (as Braithwaite suggests) some element of 'community' can be built around all individuals, that 'community' might not be strong enough nor have the required values to ensure that restorative justice works effectively. Indeed those who are most socially alienated and marginalised, those suffering the most from economic hardship, those who are most at risk from mental illness or disability, are the least

---

[112] M Umbreit and B Vos, 'Homicide Survivors Meet the Offender Prior to Execution' (2000) 4 *Homicide Studies* 63.

[113] Pavlich, above n 9, at 97.

[114] Bottoms, above n 15.

likely to be able to present themselves as suitable candidates for a restorative justice meeting. It seems to me that there is a remarkable disjuncture between the 'communities of fate' of the professional or sporting association (the type of examples provided by Braithwaite) and the 'communities of fate' of the homeless and mentally ill who move in and out of criminal justice systems through a revolving door.

Within restorative justice there are implicit consensual notions of civil society and community. But community is not a natural set of relations between individuals, nor a natural social process lying at the foundation of civil society. Communities are always constructed on the broad terrain of history and politics. Because communities are socially constructed they are also reflective and constitutive of power, difference, inequality, and potentially exploitative social and economic relations. Furthermore, community is also fundamentally about *exclusion*. The promise of community's free and un-coerced collective association is 'offset by a tendency to shore up limits, fortify a given identity, and rely on exclusion to secure self-preservation'.[115] Such a vision of community is only a short step away from the closed, gated community of the wealthy excluding the poor; the community of interest generated by power and prestige. The ideal of the community can easily spill over into class, cultural and racial purity, xenophobia and racism.[116] Indeed, the problem is that restorative justice can become what it opposes: a practice which excludes individuals because they are without community or without the *right* community.

What of the claim that restorative justice provides an avenue for 'the community' to take back from the state the ownership of the problem of crime? From feminist perspectives the problem has been that the state has never adequately criminalised violence against women. To the extent that we can discuss 'community' in this context, we may well find that 'community' reflects the patriarchal relations which provide for the acceptance of violence against

[115] Pavlich, above n 9, at 3.
[116] Z Bauman, *Globalization: the human consequences* (New York, Columbia University Press, 1998).

women. Rather than providing a barrier and safeguard against offending, it may provide social and cultural legitimation for violence. The relationship between state and community is highly complex. From a post-colonial perspective, colonial policies were directly responsible for the destruction and reconstruction of 'community' in the interests of the coloniser. Many contemporary indigenous and native communities were created directly as a result of colonial government policies of forced relocation of peoples onto various types of reservations, which were later to become designated as communities. Further, contemporary racial and ethnic minority communities within first-world nations are created under conditions determined by neo- and post-colonial relations which influence the nature of immigration and post-immigration experiences.[117] History and contemporary politics have shaped both indigenous and post-war immigrant communities. What, then, does 'community' mean for minority people in these situations, and how does it impact on relations with the police, the criminal justice system and the state more generally?

We have noted previously the tendency in late modern societies for processes which require the responsibilisation of individuals, families and communities, and the preference for 'governing at a distance'. Rose's analysis of the connection between liberal communitarian approaches, like restorative justice, and the idea of 'government through community' is particularly apt.[118] He notes that

> [a] sector is brought into existence whose vectors and forces can be mobilised, enrolled, deployed in novel programmes and techniques which encourage and harness active practices of self management and identity construction, of personal ethics and collective allegiances.[119]

Such a description could have been written precisely for the role of restorative justice. The reality of social divisions is overcome

---

[117] Cunneen and Stubbs, above n 85.

[118] N Rose, *Powers of Freedom: Reframing Political Thought* (Cambridge, Cambridge University Press, 1999).

[119] *Ibid*, at 176.

through an appeal to the common civic duties and responsibilities of citizens. Restorative justice as a social practice seeks to mobilise individuals as responsible citizens willing to engage in a communitarian ritual of apology and forgiveness. The community of restorative justice practice is constituted by the state, which designs, creates, funds and staffs the restorative justice project. It provides authority and legitimacy to the community that then participates in the restorative justice project. Such a community is not independent of state agency.[120]

There is a need for a multi-layered understanding of the problematic relationship between community and state. Restorative justice valorises the notion of 'community', which prioritises a homogeneous and consensual view of social life. While the emphasis on connection and social solidarity is appealing, this needs to be coupled with an understanding of social division. Social solidarity does not come into being simply through the application of a normative theory like restorative justice. Many communities are characterised by social exclusion, coercion and inequalities of power. Further, the application of the notion of community may serve to exclude those defined as outside the boundaries. It can serve to delegitimise and de-historicise social conflict and political struggle: political struggles which may be aimed at challenging powerful social groups who control the parameters of 'community consensus', and who exercise a 'moral authority' in their own interests.

E. Transitional Justice

Post-conflict transitional societies also have been seen as ripe for the development of large-scale restorative justice processes. Yet the evidence of the success of these approaches has been mixed. In many respects the application of restorative justice in transitional societies highlights in a concentrated form the complex intersection between law, state and community—perhaps more so than similar application in liberal democracies, where at least some level

---

[120] Pavlich, above n 9, at 97.

of legitimacy might be inferred. Restorative justice has sought to find itself an expanded role in the search for responses to mass violations of human rights and other state and civil conflicts. One part of this search has been the growing global importance of reparations for historical injustices, and the potential links between reparations and restorative justice.[121] Internationally there has been growing acceptance that governments should acknowledge and make reparations to the victims of human rights abuses, as well as widespread acceptance of the principle of reparations. Reparations have significant potential overlap with the goals of restorative justice, and have been so articulated in, for example, the South African Truth and Reconciliation Commission (SATRC). The institutionalisation of restorative justice within processes for responding to state violations of human rights can be seen in the work of organisations like the International Centre for Transitional Justice (ICTJ) in New York. The ICTJ provides advice and models for the establishment of truth and reconciliation commissions. The concern is that these processes for restorative justice are imposed, partly in the interests of the West, to resolve conflict in a particular way, and without local and organic links to the particular society.

In the field of transitional justice there is also a degree of myth-making and opportunism when it comes to the role of restorative justice. While there may be some cross-over between 'local justice' mechanisms and principles of restorative justice, a tendency has also been noted to ignore the extent to which traditional processes may be invented traditions, and to romanticise local justice processes by downplaying coercive aspects and domination by political elites. The *gacaca* courts in post-genocide Rwanda highlight some of these issues. While the Rwandan Government was faced with a task of dealing with enormous numbers of detainees as a result of the genocide through a criminal justice system incapable

---

[121] M Findlay and R Henham, *Transforming International Criminal Justice* (Devon, Willan Publishing, 2005); C Cunneen, 'Exploring the Relationship Between Reparations, the Gross Violations of Human Rights, and Restorative Justice' in D Sullivan and L Tift (eds), *The Handbook of Restorative Justice. Global Perspectives* (New York, Routledge, 2006).

of responding to the enormity of the problem, these local mechanisms of *gacaca* were never intended to deal with the sorts of severe crimes related to genocide, nor to meet the complex political and historical conditions arising from such a conflict. In post-genocide Rwanda, *gacaca* courts were redefined with a purpose of reducing the numbers of people incarcerated. In the past, *gacaca* was a system in which community elders (older men) adjudicated family and inter-family disputes over property, inheritance, personal injury or marital relations. They did not deal with serious crimes and relied on community-based forms of restitution. Punishment was not individualised. In 1999, the Government decided to modernise *gacaca*, and the 2001 *Gacaca* Law legislated for the operation of the courts. *Gacaca* courts have been re-invented as part of the state criminal justice system applying codified law, judging serious crime, using elected members and a range of penalties. In his analysis of *gacaca*, Waldorf concludes that the process is not 'participative justice': people are coerced into confessions or remaining silent; truth-telling is contingent.[122]

> Testifying in *gacaca* is necessarily subject to 'the micropolitics of local social standing'. In small face-to-face communities, giving evidence or remaining silent is more a demonstration of partisan loyalty to kin and patrons than a matter of telling the truth.[123]

Many commentators have noted that *gacaca* has been imposed by a centralised and authoritarian regime onto local communities, and that it tends to work in favour of the Tutsi and against the Hutu. The state has used coercion to operate the system, and people fear sanctions and retaliation if they do not participate.

> [T]he Rwandan government made a fundamental mistake: it warped 'customary' *gacaca* beyond recognition by converting local, ad hoc practices into more formal, coercive state structures and expanding gacaca's jurisdiction to cover genocide and crimes against humanity when, historically, it was not competent to handle serious crimes. The

---

[122] L Waldorf, 'Mass Justice for Mass Atrocity: Rethinking Local Justice as Transitional Justice' (2006) 79 *Temple Law Review* 1.
[123] *Ibid*, at 70.

government then compounded *gacaca*'s difficulties by failing to provide reparations to genocide survivors, making it an exercise in victor's justice, coercing participation, restricting freedom of speech on sensitive subjects, and collectivising guilt.[124]

More broadly used than localised processes like *gacaca*, truth commissions have been presented as a restorative justice process which capture the ideals of reconciliation, communitarianism and the establishment of truth. However, the question remains: How successful have they been in responding effectively to civil unrest and ethnic and racial conflict? A number of commentators have suggested that the international community has found it convenient to develop a restorative justice mythology around the effectiveness of truth commissions and their connection to customary forms of justice. The SATRC shows some of the problems around myth-making and the expected outcomes of restorative justice in a transitional setting. It was part of a political settlement between the National Party and the ANC, where the only viable political alternatives appeared to be complete or conditional amnesty.[125] Despite the hype, the SATRC was the product of a backroom political deal to grant amnesty to perpetrators of gross human rights abuses, which were 'defined narrowly so as to exclude lawful enforcement of apartheid'.[126]

The SATRC was an instrument within a political settlement, not an example of African dispute resolution or traditional restorative justice. It became overladen with religious and restorative justice vocabulary because of the involvement of Desmond Tutu, and it was his leadership which transformed the SATRC into a showcase for restorative justice. It was Tutu who claimed that the SATRC was a triumph of African restorative justice over Western retributive justice. As discussed previously, these binary categories are

---

[124] *Ibid*, at 84.

[125] O Lin, 'Demythologizing Restorative Justice: South African's Truth and Reconciliation Commission and Rwanda's Gacaca Courts in Context' (2006) 12 *ILSA Journal of International and Comparative Law* 41.

[126] Waldorf, above n 122, at 19.

simplistic; and as Waldorf has noted, such 'claims that particular cultural traditions promote harmony are not merely essentialist, they often serve modern political interests'.[127] In the South African case, those political interests related to achieving a broad post-apartheid political settlement. The SATRC was not connected to local community justice, and reflected state interests in reducing legal pluralism and achieving greater centralisation.

In section II. of this essay I discussed the transfer of restorative justice among first world nations. Truth commissions and their valorisation of restorative justice are also part of the global institutional environment which impacts on the choices made by transitional societies. Despite the fact that South Africans do not necessarily share the international community's uncritical devotion to the SATRC, the model has developed an apparently universal authority and legitimacy, and states are following the SATRC format despite the fact that it may be ineffective or inappropriate. There is now a dominant script for truth and reconciliation commissions, largely developed by the ICTJ and transported globally. The outcomes of this script have not always been positive—particularly where it restricts the inclusion of grassroots preferences.[128] Countries in transition are being encouraged to develop a truth and reconciliation commission because of their need for international support and aid. The effect of these economic pressures to adopt a particular transitional strategy is not only a more categorical acceptance of truth commissions, but also the perpetuation of a mythology of change, which may be ill-suited to the local needs.[129] The 'one size fits all' approach to truth and reconciliation commissions, underpinned by the claims to universalism of restorative justice, may be undermining participatory democracy rather than encouraging it. As Lundy and McGovern have succinctly stated:

---

[127] *Ibid.*

[128] J Cavallaro and S Albuja, 'The Lost Agenda: Economic Crimes and Truth Commissions in Latin America and Beyond' in K McEvoy and L McGregor (eds), *Transitional justice from below: grassroots activism and the struggle for change* (Hart Publishing Oxford, 2008).

[129] Lin, above n 125.

The attempt to apply values uniformly across cultures and societies, where the possibilities for people in those societies to participate, influence and impact upon that process are confined and delimited, is in essence a negation of those values by the very means of their supposed implementation. Put another way, the values and ideas informing justice may need to be articulated within and by each community, based on its specific realities and needs, for both conceptual and, indeed, practical reasons.[130]

Indeed it would appear that informal processes, such as restorative justice in Northern Ireland and the truth and reconciliation commission in Timor Leste, have been more effective when they have had a greater organic connection to localised processes and participation. In Timor Leste, the Community Reconciliation Process held local truth and reconciliation hearings based on local dispute resolution practices.[131] In Northern Ireland there was also a connection to local needs. The community-based restorative justice projects which developed there were established and operated independently of the state. The programs filled a vacuum in state power and had organic links to community activism, 'representing a truly grass roots response to local problems with crime and anti-social behaviour'.[132]

The point that links the discussion of restorative justice in transitional societies with its use in established liberal democracies is the problematic relationship with the state and the highly ambiguous relationship to community. Restorative justice has been primarily an add-on to existing and increasingly punitive criminal justice policies in the West, and a top-down process in transitional societies, where it is increasingly demanded by international western-dominated agencies. Restorative justice has not been a counterweight to increased punitiveness in North America, Australia, New Zealand, the UK and many parts of Europe, neither

---

[130] P Lundy and M McGovern, 'The Role of Community in Participatory Transitional Justice' in McEvoy and McGregor, above n 128, at 102.

[131] E Stanley, *Torture, Truth and Justice: the Case of Timor-Leste* (Milton Park, Routledge, 2009).

[132] A Ericksson, *Justice in Transition: Community Restorative Justice in Northern Ireland* (Devon, Willan Publishing, 2009) xvii.

has it grown in isolation from these broader trends in penality. Indeed, there has been an increased bifurcation between low-risk community-based options, like restorative justice, and more punitive trends. The bifurcation has been asymmetrical to the extent that the greatest growth has been in the harsher ends of the penal system—more people in gaol for longer periods of time.

V. CONCLUSION: SEARCHING FOR TRUTH IN RESTORATIVE JUSTICE

I want to conclude this essay with some comments on where I see restorative justice today. This essay has not sought to provide a comprehensive overview of all the possible criticisms of restorative justice. There are many potential areas of critique which could rightfully constitute a book in themselves—including, for example, questions around proportionality, just deserts and due process. What I have sought to do in this essay is to explore the wider question of the development, acceptance and contemporary place of restorative justice. These broader questions go to the heart of restorative justice's claims for legitimacy. Restorative justice advocates have never been happy with seeing restorative justice as just another criminal justice practice—they have always demanded much more, including the view that restorative justice is a *social movement*. Does the proliferation of restorative justice practice mean that it is making a significant inroad into criminal justice policy and practice? Does the 'new way of thinking' reflect an intellectual interest in a set of ideas and a significant impact on penal practices?[133] Or does O'Malley's assessment a decade ago have even greater purchase now than when it was made, that in most jurisdictions where restorative justice has a presence, it really has only a 'toehold' in practice.[134] As we move into the second decade

---

[133] G Johnstone, *Restorative Justice: Ideas, Values, Debates* (Devon, Willan Publishing, 2002) ix.

[134] P O'Malley, 'Criminologies of Catastrophe? Understanding Criminology on the Edge of the New Millennium' (2000) 33 *Australian and New Zealand Journal of Criminology* 153.

of the twenty-first century, perhaps Blagg's description of restorative justice as a good idea 'whose time has gone' is the most fitting.[135] There is no doubt that restorative justice has led to a proliferation of discussion, writing and ideas, but has it changed criminal justice practice?

Despite all the words that have been written on restorative justice over the last 25 years, one cannot escape the feeling that restorative justice is essentially a peripheral add-on to the main workings of the criminal justice system. In New South Wales, Australia, where I have lived and worked over the last two decades, there is much talk about restorative justice, and a very well-developed system of justice conferencing for young people. It is established in legislation. It has a dedicated team of conference managers and local conference convenors. There are clearly articulated legislative and administrative procedures for the use of conferences. The system has been in place since the later 1990s, developed after various trials of restorative justice for young people which date back to the early 1990s. The scheme has been positively evaluated, showing modest benefits in reduction of re-offending compared to court. So after nearly 20 years, what has been the net outcome? Depending on the year, between 2 and 4 per cent of police interventions involving young people result in referral to a youth justice conference. Police prefer all other forms of intervention, including police warnings, cautions, infringement notices (on-the-spot fines), summons to appear in court, or legal process by way of arrest and charge. Indeed the real growth during this period has been in the use of infringement notices by police against young people for a range of typically minor public order offences. In hindsight, while a small army of criminologists has been discussing and arguing the merits of restorative justice, police have decided that the most efficient way of dealing with young offenders completely dispenses with remorse, denunciation, victims, legal hearings and sentencing; it is far easier simply to write out a ticket and enforce a monetary payment. At the other end of the legal process—the courts—restorative justice has not faired any

---

[135] H Blagg, Crime, *Aboriginality and the Decolonization of Justice* (Annandale, Hawkins Press, 2008).

better. For every one young person who appears in a restorative justice conference, about 15 appear in court, and the great growth area in court has been an expanding use of incarceration both for those sentenced to imprisonment and those held on remand awaiting hearing. And this is in a jurisdiction viewed as one of the pioneers in the 1990s in developing restorative justice practice for young people.

At one level it might be argued that restorative justice is irrelevant to contemporary criminal justice systems. However, the argument of this essay is that restorative justice does indeed 'fit' within broader changes in criminal justice. It has a 'common sense' element to it, particularly in the way it reinforces crime as an individual pathology, ignores criminalisation and reduces all complexity to two parties, the offender and the victim, who are essentially unambiguous and uncomplicated individuals devoid of social characteristics. The strongly moralistic flavour of restorative justice sits well with both communitarian approaches stressing reintegration of the wrongdoing offender and the wronged victim, and conservatism that wishes to emphasise individual responsibility and moral culpability. The social connectedness and moral certainty provided by restorative justice plays an important function in securing consent to a justice system which is largely devoid of either of these two features. Restorative justice represents itself as an ethically preferred model of doing justice: it is an inherently *good thing* to do. The claims of restorative justice to a pre-state authenticity and universalism support the commonsense appeal: restorative justice is *naturally* superior to legal-bureaucratic forms of justice and it is a universal process available to all people. Yet at the same time, paradoxically, restorative justice conceals both law and the state, both of which are embodied in all that restorative justice does. Even the day-to-day script of restorative justice is dissembling because of the widespread absence of actual victims and their replacement by a quasi-representative of the state (the convenor).

What of restorative justice as a normative theory? Is a normative theory enough for those academics and individuals working in the criminal justice system who desire systemic change? And, given the types of problems identified in this essay, is restorative justice sufficient as a normative theory? Daly questions the 'nirvana story' of restorative justice which, she suggests, 'helps us to imagine what is possible, but . . . should not be used as the benchmark for what is practical and achievable'.[136] But surely this is exactly what is required if we are to transform the criminal justice system? The significant limitation of restorative justice as a normative theory is that it does not engage with current restorative justice practices and the broader functions of the criminal justice system. In other words, restorative justice lacks *praxis*—in the sense of a constantly reflexive, dialectical relationship between theory and action. It lacks an analysis of its own significant shortcomings; it lacks an analysis of political power and social power; it lacks a transformative politics.

The shift in restorative justice claims over the last two decades reflects this problem. In the 1990s, restorative justice was heralded as nothing less than a social movement aimed at change. Today its academic advocates have moved from accepting a responsibility for political analysis of the intersections between criminalisation, law and the state, and the place of restorative justice in contemporary criminal justice systems, to a position of arguing that restorative justice is a normative theory. Reducing restorative justice to a theory of *what should be*, in the absence of a thorough-going analysis of *what is*, means that restorative justice is bound to fail as a transformative social movement. Perhaps we should focus on those that restorative justice has failed the most. Despite all the claims about pre-state justice, it has certainly failed indigenous youth, whose over-representation in prison has been increasing. This not only undermines theoretical claims about the origins of restorative justice in indigenous practices, but also clearly demonstrates the failure of restorative justice theorists and practitioners to analyse the racial impacts of the criminal justice system.

One of the foundational claims of restorative justice is that truth is obscured through legal processes of the criminal justice system, and that restorative justice can better establish the 'truth'. But what

---

[136] Daly, above n 2, at 234.

is the truth that restorative justice seeks to establish? Do we mean by truth the 'facts'—the facts, for example, of the crime? Legal processes also establish fact; and while the rules of evidence construct truth within particular parameters, there is no reason to suspect that these truths will be any less or more factual than the truth constructed by restorative justice. As noted, in most cases these facts are not going to be in dispute. Truth, of course, has other connotations. Perhaps it is 'meaning' which restorative justice seeks to establish in a way which is superior to court processes— the *meaning* of the crime to the victim and the offender. Perhaps it is an older idea of truth—being true to oneself and sincere—to which restorative justice advocates are referring when they suggest that truth is a prerequisite for forgiveness and reconciliation.[137] Yet the meaning which restorative justice establishes is not divorced from social contexts, it is not the simplistic, individualised expression of guilt, forgiveness and restoration which permeates restorative justice literature. At best, truth is partial and contingent wherever it is constructed. Both criminal justice and restorative justice involve truth-seeking processes, and the end-product of neither should be seen as an objective reflection of reality. Part of the purpose of this essay has been to identify the particular elements which comprise the restorative justice's 'regime of truth'. Perhaps restorative justice simulates something which never really existed—a kind of hyper-reality of the justice system which is fair and equitable and offering redemption for all; where offenders are free agents who are now contrite; where victims are engaged civic personalities who forgive and forget. And, in practice, restorative justice appears endlessly malleable by those social activists and practitioners who genuinely desire a better outcome for both offenders and victims, politicians who find restorative justice in the public humiliation of offenders, and evangelical supporters who advocate the use of restorative justice everywhere, even in death penalty cases.

---

[137] J Doak, *Victims' Rights, Human Rights and Criminal Justice: Re-conceiving the Role of Third Parties* (Oxford, Hart Publishing, 2008) 263.

Index

Lightning Source UK Ltd.
Milton Keynes UK
UKOW05f1126311013

220168UK00004B/19/P